AF581072

The Solo Honeymoon

The Solo Honeymoon

A BRIEF BEAUTIFUL TRUE LOVE STORY

Laura Murphy

with Bret Witter

DUTTON

An imprint of Penguin Random House LLC
1745 Broadway, New York, NY 10019
penguinrandomhouse.com

Book design by Nancy Resnick
Illustrations by Alexis C. Seabrook

LIBRARY OF CONGRESS CATALOGING-IN-PUBLICATION DATA

has been applied for.

ISBN 9798217177257 (hardcover)
ISBN 9798217177264 (ebook)

Printed in the United States of America
1st Printing

The authorized representative in the EU for product safety and compliance is Penguin Random House Ireland, Morrison Chambers, 32 Nassau Street, Dublin D02 YH68, Ireland, https://eu-contact.penguin.ie.

For Devon.

You always wanted me to write a book. It shouldn't have happened this way.

The Solo Honeymoon

Anyone who knows me knows I am not one for speeches. I actually wrote a speech in junior high about why I hate giving speeches. But if there is anyone in the world who could get me up here, it's Devon.

Devon didn't know this, but that was actually the opening to a speech I was planning to give at our wedding.

May 19, 2024

Devon's Celebration of Life

Before

I HAD WANTED to go to Castellina in Chianti, Italy, for years. My fiancé Devon's father vacationed there every fall, and Devon had shared with me his family photographs of narrow cobblestoned streets, close-packed medieval buildings, and long gorgeous views over rolling Tuscan hills. I had watched Devon grow up in those photographs, from a teenager in ill-fitting shorts to the kind, handsome, fun-loving man I had fallen in love with. I had seen his happiness blossom over time; a happiness the two of us were eager to share for the rest of our lives. So the village was an obvious destination when we sat down together to choose locations in Europe for our honeymoon.

Still, I was surprised by Castellina. I had come from London, a modern and boisterous city, and the village was a contrast: ancient, peaceful, and more intimate than any social media post or photograph could capture. From every angle there was a gorgeous view: an alley twisting between two yellow stucco buildings; a glimpse of formal gardens across a courtyard; an ancient tower above terra-cotta roofs. The palazzo where Devon's father rented an apartment was near the top of the hill, with the vineyards of Tuscany spreading out to the horizon below it; vineyards I had seen in the background of so many photos of the man I loved. You know love at the moment you experience it. It's an electricity that thrills you, a peace that cools and calms. I fell in love with Devon a few weeks into our friendship, as we sat on a cliff watching the sun rise over the ocean. I fell in love with Castellina as I watched an older couple walking arm in arm, helping each other along its uneven streets.

The sunset, though, is what you come to a place like Castellina for. Already on my honeymoon I had spent a day on the French Riviera. I climbed a mountain in Ireland. I went backstage at a West End musical. I ate dinner while hovering twenty feet above the Mediterranean Sea. All those experiences should have been magical. They should have been luminous, like my mad dash to the ideal spot to watch the sun drift down below the Tuscan hills. Instead, each of those moments was shot through with sadness because Devon wasn't there. My fiancé, the love of my life, the best person I have ever known, died in my arms one month before our wedding, and I was on our honeymoon alone.

I never thought I'd write this book. A year ago, I was a twenty-seven-year-old associate lawyer at a small firm in my small hometown a thousand miles from anywhere. I had two dogs, a three-bedroom house, and a fiancé I was madly in love with, and who was madly in love with me. I was happy. I know that sounds simplistic, but that was my story: I was happy, and nobody gets asked to write about being happy. My life might not have been perfect—whose is?—but I was perfectly content.

Then Devon died, and my life shattered into a billion pieces, like the exploding of a sun.

Everything I've done since that moment has been about that moment, this sometimes frantic, sometimes crawling attempt to pull myself together. Clinging to memories of Devon, terrified I'll begin to forget. Pushing away the pain because I'm drowning in it. I took a leave of absence from my job. I took a leave of absence from my life. I spent three months in a sadness so black I couldn't eat. I couldn't get out of bed, because there was nothing that interested me, no place I wanted to go, no future without the future I had envisioned with Devon, and the children we were supposed to have, and the sixty years we should have lived together.

I'm not going to dwell in that dark place, even though, even now, I still go there. This is not a book about my depression. It's about loss . . . and love. Friends . . . and travel. It's about just getting up and *doing* when the last thing you want to do is get out of bed.

It's about Devon, my beloved Dev, who was so much more than this tragic thing that happened to him. I want the world—I want you—to understand that. I want you to know that he was funny, that he was kind, that Devon O'Grady loved everyone, even those who didn't love him back. I want you to know that he was flawed, he made mistakes. But he was never malicious.

He was barely competent in the kitchen. But he never told me lies.

He thought it was funny to hug me long and hard when he was sweaty from a run. But he never said an unkind word to me.

He poured water into the blender and drank the last gray clumps of every smoothie. But oh my god, he was sexy when he took me in his arms and kissed me.

He broke me when he died. He broke me. But alive, he made me whole.

He was my ultimate hype-man. He believed in me.

He would have been your hype-man, too. No matter who you are, Devon would have believed in you.

I've shared pieces of our story already, in TikToks that went viral. Millions of people followed me as I flew out alone on the honeymoon Devon and I had planned. I wanted to see, as I said in my first post, if life was still worth living. Millions of people watched me search for the answer. Millions of people told me, *We're with you, Laura, we believe in you, there is so much more for you to do, for you to give.* I didn't know what to do with this generosity of spirit, this unexpected connection. For months, I had felt alone. Now I was overwhelmed by how enormous and kind the world could be. How do I answer a million voices when I am only one?

And then I thought of this: I can get off social media and dig down deep into what my love for Devon meant. I can show you how connection changes your life, how your pain is a reflection of your joy.

I'm not writing *The Year of Magical Thinking,* though this book, in part, is for those who are grieving. However hopeless you're feeling right now, however meaningless your life may seem, I've been there, too. You are not alone. You are not lost. You cannot die of heartbreak. I've written this book to prove this simple message: You can and will go on.

I am also not writing *Eat Pray Love,* although a life-affirming overseas journey is here as well. I hope you find magic and beauty in these pages.

I'm trying, I'm really trying, to write a book about love.

This book is organized around the six weeks I spent on my honeymoon alone, but it's also about the three years I spent with Devon. That time has ended now, but it's not gone. It's in my heart. It's in my mind. It changes every time I come back to the page, it grows with every word you read.

So many times I felt alone in grief. I felt so very, very alone. But the truth is, I was never alone. I had my family. I had my friends. I had the four million people on TikTok who cheered for me. I had the hundreds of young women who reached out to me from circumstances like my own. I have the tens of millions—the hundreds of millions—who have gone before and led the way, who have suffered catastrophic loss and relearned the art of vibrant living.

Even when I was sprinting toward the sunset in Castellina, I was not alone. Devon's sister, Kathleen, was beside me, running step for step. Loss, despair, the hope that begins to grow from the depths of pain: This is the human condition. The eternal story and struggle. It's not just me. It's not just everyone who loved Devon. It's all of us.

I'm nobody special. To the rest of the world, Devon was nobody special. But he was special to me. All I can tell you is this: You want to love someone the way that I loved Devon. You want to be loved the way Devon loved me.

In the end, that's why I'm writing this book. Because we're all running to catch that perfect sunset, to capture the brilliant flare of love before it drops into the sea.

London

THEY SAY IT'S hard to know where to start a story, but for me it's easy. I'm going to start at the top, on the day I first saw Devon, because that's when everything changed for me, and it's a classic meet-cute straight out of Emily Henry or Jane Austen. And also, somehow, exactly who we are.

It happened in the depths of the Covid winter. I was going to law school at Dalhousie University, in Halifax, Nova Scotia, because there are no law schools on the island of Newfoundland, where I was born and raised. I was home for Christmas vacation when a Covid outbreak struck Halifax and the law school went online. I needed to find a law internship for the summer—articling, as we call it in Canada—so I sent my résumé to several law offices in St. John's, the largest city in Newfoundland. The oldest firm on the island liked what they saw. They asked me to come in for an interview.

Newfoundland, which together with Labrador forms a province, is an island off the northeast coast of Canada. It is 42,000 square miles in area, roughly the same size as Bulgaria or the state of Virginia. It is the sixteenth-largest island in the world. It has a population of about five hundred thousand—less than twelve people per square mile. Half of that population lives in or near St. John's on the Avalon Peninsula, which hangs off the extreme southeastern corner of the island. My hometown, Corner Brook, is on the west coast of Newfoundland. It is a seven-hour drive on the Trans-Canada Highway—the only road across the island—from Corner Brook to St. John's, and there's not much out there except trees, moose, and the occasional Tim Hortons.

I told them I was happy to drive over and interview in person.

I set up three interviews in St. John's. A lawyer from the second firm, Curtis Dawe, emailed the morning of the interview and said the elevator was out, to call her before I arrive and she'd meet me in the lobby. The first interview ran long, so I was late. I was literally running down Water Street, the main road in downtown St. John's. That's when I realized my phone had died because of the subzero temperature. It was an older model; it struggled to handle the Newfoundland winter.

When I reached the building, there was nobody in the lobby. There wasn't even a desk or directory. No phone. I stood there for a few minutes, unsure what to do, until a woman came in carrying a Curtis Dawe bag. With the elevator out, she said, we'd have to take the stairs. The office was on the twelfth floor. The tallest building in Newfoundland is fifteen stories. Only six buildings in the whole province have twelve floors.

The woman, who was older, didn't make it. She stopped to rest on the sixth floor. She told me to go on, and I am ashamed to say I left her in that concrete shaft and hustled up the last six flights on my own. I was wearing my heavy winter coat and a leather backpack. By the time I got to the twelfth floor, I was drenched in sweat.

The door was locked. I thought that was odd until I realized this was a fire escape, not a normal staircase, and this was an emergency door.

I started pounding on it. Nothing. I thought about being trapped in the stairwell, of having to walk back down, and I realized I should have asked to use that woman's phone, or I should have waited for my phone to warm up. I never should have gone into a dimly lit concrete shaft with no plan except to pound frantically on a metal door until I was not only sweating but out of breath.

And then someone opened the door.

It was Devon. I won't say it was love at first sight, because it wasn't. We were wearing masks. All we could see was each other's eyes. Devon had gorgeous blue eyes.

And he looked good in a suit. He was trim and tailored. He had flowing brown hair that curled up at his collar. He wore circular glasses. He had far more style than your average Newfoundland lawyer.

I'm sure he went out of his way to not only take me to my meeting, but to make me feel like I was right on time (I was twenty minutes late), looking sharp, and perfect for the job. I can't remember a word he said, but that's Devon. Positive. Reassuring. Always kind.

I didn't see him after the interview, but I checked the firm's website as soon as my phone decided to un-die. I couldn't find his photograph, and I couldn't remember his name. I figured he was a temporary employee, maybe an intern, which meant he might not be there in the summer, even if I got the job.

Two hours after the interview, Curtis Dawe offered me a position. I blew off my last interview and accepted it right away, because I loved the firm. And sure enough, the first person I saw on my first day in the office four months later was that stylish young lawyer who had opened the door and rescued me from my foolishness.

"Backpack Girl!" he yelled. That was Devon's nickname for me.

I could see the other associates chuckling, but it took a week before one admitted, "Yeah, we were wondering about you, Backpack Girl. He'd been asking about you for months."

I HAVE A confession: I'm not brave. I'm determined. I work hard, and I achieve. But I don't fling myself at adventures. I don't make the first move. Going on my honeymoon alone, that certainly wasn't brave, like everyone seems to think. It was, if I'm being honest, closer to fear.

I went into shock when Devon died. That's the only way to say it. His death was so sudden, so unexpected, that my body shut down. My mind collapsed. In an instant, the life I had and the future I saw were shattered. I'd come out of a fog of grief that could last for hours or even days, and I'd think that maybe it didn't happen, it couldn't be, and I'd realize no, it happened, Devon is gone, and I'd plunge into an even deeper level of darkness: more pain, more depression, less desire. I didn't want to get out of bed. I didn't want to shower. I wanted to lie still, thinking about Devon. Looking at pictures of Devon in my camera roll. Writing him messages in the Notes app on my phone.

It hurts so much tonight. I want to die, too.

There will never be anything better than the comfort and love I felt with you.

What can I do for you? I'm sorry. I miss you so much. I love you more than the world. I'm trying to understand. I don't know what to do. What would you want me to do?

There's a difference between being suicidal and not wanting to live. That's what my family and friends didn't understand. They were afraid for me, but I never intended to let go. I only wanted the wave to come and wash me away, to take me under and drown me in the sea.

But eventually, I, too, began to worry. I started to feel that if I didn't get up soon, I would never get up. Every morning, I told myself, This is the day. And yet the thought of walking down the stairs and seeing my family nervously watching me from the sofa. Of walking out into my small hometown, where everyone knew what happened. Of going to a grocery store where everyone would stare at me, wonder about me, pity me.

I need you here to hold me, I wrote to Devon. *Only you.*

That space of grief is a deep, dark pit. The walls are steep. I didn't know how to pull myself out, and I wasn't sure I wanted to try. But I had one concrete thing in my future, one handhold that felt close enough to grab: a one-way airplane ticket to London, the first stop on the honeymoon that Devon and I were only in the beginning stages of planning.

And I wanted to go. To escape to a place where no one knew

my name. Where no one knew what had happened. I wanted to be in the places Devon and I would have visited, doing the things we would have done.

I wanted to stay home and curl around his memory in the bed we bought and the home we made.

My mind was jagged. I want to go. I want to stay. I need to go. I didn't have the strength to do anything but stay.

I was terrified of leaving the safety of my family and friends while in such a depressed, near catatonic state. What if my depression worsened overseas? But in the end, I was more afraid of never trying, of passing on my one clear chance to pull myself out of the great black void that was slowly, relentlessly pulling me down.

"I'm going," I told my father the night before the plane was scheduled to leave.

But in the morning, I lost my way, and I couldn't finish packing my bags. I called my best friend Reb. "I can't do it," I said. "I'm overwhelmed."

"I'm coming over," she said. She gathered my toiletries. She chose a few last outfits. She made sure I had my passport and my comfy airplane clothes. I didn't feel like I was there. I didn't feel like I was making a decision. It felt more like some tidal force was taking me.

It was only later that my friends and family told me: "That was so brave, Laura. We can't believe you did it. We never thought you'd go."

I SAW DEVON in the office every day. I worked on the eleventh floor, he worked on the twelfth, but we always seemed to bump into each other.

"You look nice today," he'd say. "That's a great fit."

Devon wore slim-fitting suits with a vest. A vest! He owned dress shoes but mostly wore sneakers—and pulled the whole look off. He owned at least three pairs of glasses. (I learned later it was six.) He was interested in fashion. He noticed what people were wearing and referred to it as a *fit* or a *piece*. As in, "That's a nice piece, Backpack Girl. What brand is that?"

"Oh, um, it's Aritzia." I had bought three of their pantsuits before starting work.

"It looks great on you."

"Okay . . . thanks."

I guess? I wasn't sure how to take the compliments. We don't get complimented much in modern life, especially in public, and especially not with Devon's casual sincerity. But slowly, surely, the kindness boosts your confidence, and I needed that. This internship was a tryout for my dream career, and I was putting a lot of pressure on myself to be perfect.

"You're doing a great job," Devon would say, and I'd think, How do you know?

Then he'd mention something specific, and I'd realize he *was* paying attention, and not just to my fit. Devon was finishing his year of articling, a post-grad requirement in Canada before you are licensed as a lawyer. He had a lot of work. And yet, he seemed to know everything about my office life.

It wasn't personal, though. Devon said kind things to everyone. He had nicknames for everyone in the office: "Son" for Sonya; "Shawn" for Shawna; "Seagull" for Frankie. I was intimidated by Amy, the firm's managing partner, but Devon joked with her like they were longtime friends. I'd hear him almost every day chatting with Sandra, aka "San," whose cubicle was outside my office. San ate questionable lunches, like SpaghettiOs and potted meat.

"What do you have for lunch today, San?" I'd hear Devon say, not in a mean way, but like he was interested in her, and they had private jokes.

"Oh, you know. What about you?"

When I heard her laughing, I'd look out my door and see Devon biting into a green pepper as if it were an apple. Or chomping the end off a raw cucumber. Or peeling the leaves off a head of romaine lettuce and stuffing them in his mouth. San wasn't the weird one; Devon was the weird one. That was the joke. Everyone made fun of his raw vegetable lunches, but he didn't care. He was comfortable with who he was.

On Fridays, the associates gathered for drinks at the Salt House, a restaurant a few blocks down Water Street. It was May, so it was rainy and cold. Newfoundland doesn't get warm until June. But Covid had finally tired itself out, or the world had finally gotten tired of dealing with it, so the restaurants were open. I sat on the edge of the group. I loved everyone at the office, I was making friends, but I was still the new girl. Devon was at the center of everything. He was always talking. But his jokes and stories never felt selfish. He was more the leader of the conversation. With a few words, a quick joke, he would bring people in, make them feel noticed.

And when he looked at me, it was like a light. I could feel the heat, something coming alive. It wasn't long before I found myself coming up with excuses to drift by his office.

But he was just out of a relationship, and I was serious about my law career. I didn't want the distraction of dating a coworker, even if it was allowed, and I wasn't sure it was, so why take the risk, even if Devon O'Grady looked incredible in his three-piece suits and sneakers?

And besides, I wasn't special to him. Devon made everyone feel special, that's all.

I BECAME SUSPICIOUS—intrigued—when Devon started to message me recipes for gluten-free breads and pastries. He wasn't gluten-free. He was a *raw vegetable eater.* No one would touch gluten-free baked goods if they weren't on a gluten-free diet, so I knew Devon was searching out those recipes for me.

I BROKE DOWN in tears at the steak restaurant in the international terminal of the Montreal airport. I pulled out my laptop and drowned my sorrow in wine (exactly what my therapist warned me not to do) and a murder documentary (to keep things light).

I broke down again on the plane to London when my seat didn't come with a screen. Have you ever cried over a screen? Probably. We're living in the age of screens. Devon loved low-stakes comedies: *The Office, Superstore*. He devoured basketball highlights on his phone. I preferred to read. I was in the middle of *The Invisible Life of Addie LaRue* when Devon died. I hadn't been able to read a page since. Murder documentaries filled the void. I watched them incessantly. People say they're trash; I disagree. They matter because they're real.

What was I going to do on an eight-hour flight without *American Murder: Laci Peterson*?

I took out one of Devon's sweatshirts and draped it over my chest, then wrapped the arms around me like a hug. It was his favorite: the one with Muhammad Ali's face on the back. I clutched Muhammad Ali to my chest and, thankfully, fell asleep. It was only when I woke up for landing that I realized a screen had been in my armrest all along. Still a valid crash-out in my opinion.

An hour later, I was on the other side of customs, in a cavernous welcome area with branching hallways, a dozen doors, and an endless stream of strangers rushing past. And I couldn't figure out what to do. I had no idea what I was even supposed to be doing. My brain had been working at about ten percent capacity since Devon died, even on the best of days, but these periods of shutting down, of browning out, were common, too. Experts call it *grief brain:* a fog that descends. I stood in Heathrow for thirty minutes, according to my phone, and I can't tell you a single thing I did in all that time.

Eventually, it came to me. London. I'm in London. The Tube. The name of the hotel where I was booked for my first three nights. I bought a SIM card for my phone, found a transportation map, and boarded the train. I popped up into a cold rain—hello, London, lovely August you have here!—a few blocks from my hotel. I was proud of myself. I had traveled before, but never alone, and I'd made it through my fog into the heart of London, a city with a population nearly twenty times larger than Newfoundland's—although we clearly have them beat for moose and trees.

Take that, grief brain!

My room wasn't ready, but my hotel, the Hoxton, Holborn, was charming. I think that's the word for comfy British stuff. I had booked a hotel with a restaurant and bar in case I didn't feel like going outside. I settled in for a cappuccino.

The caffeine didn't help. As soon as they let me into my room, I collapsed into bed.

DEVON ASKED ME if I wanted to watch the sunrise. Whoa, did I hear him right? To watch the sun . . . *rise*? No one does that. The days are long in June in Newfoundland. I checked my weather app. The sun rose at 5:02 A.M. We would have to get up at 4:00 A.M. to see it. That's insane. Or utterly romantic.

I said yes, of course.

He picked me up outside my rental house. It was dark. I was barely awake, but Devon was chipper. He handed me a thermos of hot coffee and headed out. St. John's is built on a deep, narrow harbor. The downtown sits along the northern edge, with the row houses of the old town climbing up the hill behind it. On the northeastern tip of the harbor is the Battery, a collection of colorful fishing shacks and colonial-era working-class houses pressed into the foot of a steep, unbuildable promontory. That outcropping is Signal Hill, where Fort Waldegrave, raised by the British in 1798, guards the Narrows at the mouth of the harbor. Signal Hill is ten blocks from downtown, but it's a wilderness of rocks, moors, and mountain lakes that looks like the Scottish Highlands. Most people, if they were going to see the sunrise, go to Signal Hill. Most people.

Devon drove around to the south side of the harbor. There's nothing on that side but the docks, where oceangoing cargo ships unload. St. John's is the only major port in the North Atlantic for hundreds of miles. The docks are directly across from the center of the city. I could see them from our offices on Water Street. But I had never been there. I thought it was an industrial zone, and that's exactly what it was. Devon drove through the gate and into the shipping yard, where spare parts were stacked in lopsided piles and boats were leaning akimbo on their keels. It was mostly dark, with only a hint of light at the Narrows. We were alone. Where was this guy taking me?

On the far side of the shipyard was a turnaround. We parked and started walking up a narrow road closed off by a rusty chain. The road rose sharply, the surf pounding at the rocky shoreline on our left. A small group of houses was hidden around a rock outcropping, a village of maybe twenty-five people clinging to the coast.

On the far side of the last house, the cliffs closed in: a steep climb on the right, a steep drop on the left. There was nothing to see in the darkness, nothing to hear but the peaceful drone of the waves hitting the rocks eighty feet below. As the road began to curve around another promontory, Devon began to talk about Sue. She was his aunt, but like a mother to him. She had died a few years before, in her fifties, of brain cancer, and I could hear the love in his voice, the rawness of his loss. It was so shocking, I didn't know what to say. I once dated a man for two years, and he never told me anything this heartfelt or personal.

At the end of the road was a red and white lighthouse perched on a hundred-fifty-foot cliff. Fort Amherst. Devon pushed open a gate marked DO NOT ENTER, and we sat on a small patch of grass on the far side of the lighthouse. Dawn was hitting the cliffs, turning the edges of the waves bright white as they smashed to bits beneath us. We watched the sun rise over the lip of the North Atlantic without a word, the sky brightening from purple to orange to red to pinkish blue.

I didn't take a photograph. I didn't want to be distracted, to miss what was right in front of me in a futile attempt to capture it forever. But as the sun began to clear the water, Devon pulled something from his pocket. It was a small wooden heart. On it was scrawled, in sloppy silver paint, the word *time*.

It was a reference, he told me, to something his Grampy always said: Time is the most precious thing we have. Spend it wisely.

Grampy died during the pandemic, a few years after his daughter Sue. The family wasn't able to gather for his funeral, but he had given out these hearts over the years to the people he loved, and Devon always kept his heart with him.

He held it up to the sunrise and took a photograph. Maybe that seems contrived to you. It wasn't. I saw Devon hold that heart in front of a hundred special places, at a hundred special moments, and take a photograph. Time, spent wisely. Those photos must be in his phone, if I can find the strength to crack it.

We talked a lot in the coming months about his past relationships. He was honest with my questions; he was complimentary of his former girlfriends. They were good people. They were great partners. It was him, he said, not them. He tried too hard. He had sabotaged every romantic relationship that had ever meant anything to him.

And yet, he said, he had never taken a girlfriend to Fort Amherst to watch the sunrise. He had a feeling, he told me later, that I would understand him.

Devon was right. I understood perfectly well that if this was a first date, then this guy was *different*.

And I liked it.

WE DIDN'T KISS. We didn't hold hands. Sunrise may be the most romantic moment of every day, but nothing romantic happened at Fort Amherst. We sat on the edge of a cliff and let the sun wash over us. We talked about our lives. We walked back down around the promontory, the light low and long, our shadows stretched out before us. He dropped me at my house around 6:00 A.M. Even though it was a workday, it was still a quarter hour before I usually got out of bed.

I spent the next few hours showering, getting dressed, thinking about Aunt Sue, about how open Devon was with his feelings, about how thrilling it was going to be to see him, even though I didn't know his intentions, even though I wondered if—and worried that—he only thought of us as friends. I waited half the morning, completely distracted, before heading to his office.

"Backpack Girl!" I felt a warmth wash over me, like early-morning sun.

Later, I heard him joking with San about her lunch. I stepped outside my office and watched him butter up this lovely older woman, making her laugh. He turned and looked at me.

"Nice fit," he said, and I felt the heat under my skin. He had said the same thing twenty times before, but it was different now because I knew I wanted to be with him, and I wanted those words to mean he wanted to be with me.

On Friday, he asked what I was doing for the weekend. My father was in town to visit. I was having dinner with him. "I'll drive you," Devon said.

He dropped me off outside the restaurant. I didn't mention Devon by name, but my father knew, he said, by the way I smiled when he asked how I had gotten there, and I said, "A friend gave me a ride."

The next weekend, Devon went to his family's cottage. Many Newfoundlanders have second homes. It's a joke here. Newfies never pay for a dinner out, because they need the money for their snowmobile and their primitive cabin. My grandmother worked at a fish processing plant, and even she had a cottage on an inland lake. Electricity but no running water, complete tranquility, except for the banging of the pots and pans as she carried water from the lake. That's what I remember about that cabin: the endless trees, the quiet water, and the sound of my grandmother working.

On Sunday afternoon, on his way back to St. John's, Devon texted that he wanted to come by. I felt a wave of hope, of happiness, but when he arrived, he was quiet. He seemed distracted. I had been friends with the last person I dated for a year before we started seeing each other. Those months seemed half as long, and a quarter as confusing, as the ten days since Fort Amherst.

We watched television from opposite ends of the couch, barely talking. The feelings I had for Devon were so big that I knew I couldn't hold them in forever. But I couldn't speak them, either. I should have done it before, because now that so much time had passed, there was too much between us, and I was too afraid that I was wrong about what our sunrise meant.

"I need to go," Devon said, cutting the tension.

He stood up. I walked him to the door. I said good-bye.

He smiled. "See you tomorrow, Laura."

I hit the wall. I mean: I slammed backward into the wall as Devon's mouth covered mine. He might have pushed me, but I think I saw him leaning, and I pulled him in. In an instant, we were kissing deeply. This was no subtle signal of intention; it was wrestling, a struggle for a position, one second my lips on top of his, the next his lips on mine. We danced across my entrance hall, wrapped in each other's arms, until we finally unclasped, breathing heavy, and stepped apart.

I looked at him. He looked at me. His famous round glasses were knocked askew.

He opened the door without a word and left.

I WOKE UP with sunlight streaming in the window and Devon's Muhammad Ali sweatshirt hugging me, like a warm memory of mornings past. This wasn't twenty hours since I'd gone to sleep; it was closer to forty hours. The first time I woke up, it was dark, and I was hungry, so I went to a pub. I ordered a gluten-free beer. I set a goal: to talk to someone other than the waitress. I failed. I sat at my little table and watched other people laughing and chatting with their dates, their mates, their significant others. I had traveled many times before—to Europe, to Asia, to the Caribbean—but never like this. Never as an escape. Never under duress. Never alone.

Traveling alone can be a very lonely experience.

The next day, I managed to leave my room for an early dinner. I went to Wingstop because, first, it was on the same block as my hotel.

Second, my best friend Reb was obsessed with it. She spent hours on TikTok watching people eating and describing fast food. We don't have many American chains in Newfoundland, so Reb loved watching mukbangs of places like Taco Bell, Chipotle, and Raising Cane's. She was disappointed when I came back from Arizona and told her In-N-Out Burger was just okay.

And third, there was a line out the door, so I wasn't the only one eating American-style fast-food chicken wings in London.

I'll give it a six out of ten, mostly because I spent the meal FaceTiming with Reb from my hotel room. Mukbangs are always graded.

After hanging up with Reb, I started working on a TikTok. I had promised to keep my friends and family updated on my travels, and since I wasn't a frequent social media user, I figured TikTok would be the easiest way to do that. My post was one minute, eighteen seconds long. It was a series of mundane moments—the airport, the airplane, the Tube, street scenes, my food, a brief flash of my beloved murder documentaries. It took me three hours to splice it together. I was so tired by the end, I did the voice-over in one take.

"My fiancé died a month before our wedding," it started, "and now I'm going on our honeymoon alone to see if life is worth living."

ON MY THIRD day in London, I woke up early—1:18 P.M., *barely* afternoon. Grief throws you out of time, you lose yourself in memory and mourning, but the devices of the modern world will remind you of the time down to the minute.

I knew I needed to get out and experience the city, but I was struggling. Doesn't matter what you do, Laura, I told myself, just put on pants and walk out the door.

I got dressed. I had a cappuccino at the hotel lobby bar. I stepped into the street. I didn't know where to go, so I started wandering. My hotel was in a wealthy neighborhood. The streets were crowded with young and well-dressed people. This isn't Corner Brook, I thought, and that thought was comforting. So I walked. And walked. And walked.

I ended up at a place called Seven Dials Market, a high-end food court in a converted warehouse. It was packed. Music was blaring. I thought it would be easy to find a nice place to eat, but I descended into grief brain and ended up circling through the place several times before I noticed a stall selling corn tacos and margaritas, both gluten-free. I took a picture of my tacos when I sat down, so I know what time it was: 4:47 P.M. I had walked for close to three hours. I was seven blocks from my hotel.

I went back to the Hoxton after "breakfast." I didn't have the energy for anything else. I looked at photos of Devon on my phone. I watched a few videos I had taken: my "morning" coffee, a crowded street, my breakfast tacos and alcohol. I spent a few hours making a second post for my TikTok account. I wrapped myself in Devon's sweatshirt, pulled up my beloved murder documentaries, and fell asleep again.

When I woke up, it was almost midnight. I headed out to Wingstop, something haters on the internet would spend months mocking me for because they thought chicken wings were gluten bombs, even though the non-breaded ones are (mostly) gluten-free.

Tragically, the Wingstop was closed. Oh, come on, I did not have the energy for this. But then, as I was wandering down a busy street, FaceTiming with my father, I saw it, beaming out in all its ultra-yellow glory, the ultimate comfort hole . . . McDonald's.

I was standing on the corner, waiting for the walk signal, when

I noticed three girls staggering toward me. Clearly Americans, and clearly drunk.

Just do it, Laura. Just talk to them.

I suppose I should mention I was wearing pajama bottoms and Devon's Mohammad Ali sweatshirt. They were nice pajama bottoms, but they weren't appropriate for an evening stroll in central London. I didn't care. My superpower, at least for this first part of the trip, was that I didn't care about anything.

I struck up a conversation. The girls were also headed to McDonald's. We decided to go together.

The last thing everyone said to me before I left Newfoundland was, for the love of god, don't tell anyone you are a young woman traveling alone.

It took me about two minutes of dodging questions to realize that was impossible. So I told the girls I was alone, and then I told them why I was alone, and then I trauma dumped on those poor girls, right there in the harsh lights of a London McDonald's. It was the first time I had ever talked about Devon with anyone who didn't know him. I'd like to tell you it felt good or bad or . . . something, but at the time, it just felt necessary.

The girls were kind. A bit of drunken fawning, but they seemed sincerely moved. One of them invited me shopping the next day. She was on a semester abroad from a California state university, and she was living in a big building full of girls on semesters abroad from various California state universities. She wanted to go to a famous vintage boutique, so eight of us bundled onto a big red London bus. The shop was closed, so four of us decided to walk to Camden Market. Well, they decided. I tagged along.

It was clear I didn't have much in common with these girls.

They were nineteen, maybe twenty. They were focused on Instagram, legal drinking, and complaining about homesickness and boys. I was a twenty-eight-year-old widow trying to figure out how to get through a day. But they were nice. And it was nice to be with other people. And I think I fooled them. I think I came off like a normal human being.

We were walking along a fancy canal, with London hovering above us, when I happened to glance at my phone. The TikTok I posted on my second day in London had six hundred thousand views.

"Oh my god," I said. "I think my social media is blowing up."

A WEEK AFTER Devon died, I asked my father to find someone who had lost a partner at my age. My closest friends were engaged, married, or having babies. How could they understand what it was like to have those things torn violently away? To lose everything I cared about in an instant?

"I need to know," I told my father, "that it's possible to go on."

The woman he found was in her fifties. She was a grief counselor who had, in her early thirties, lost her husband in a notorious helicopter crash that killed ten workers on their way to an oil rig off the north coast. She still lived in their house, with his things. She couldn't bear the thought of selling them. She had recently started her first serious relationship since his death.

It terrified me.

No, I thought. I don't want that. I don't want to grieve for the rest of my life. I couldn't imagine loving anyone but Devon. I still can't. But still . . .

I turned to books. Joan Didion's *The Year of Magical Thinking* made my grief feel seen. *The Hot Young Widows Club* was almost the exact opposite, and almost as good. I found some comfort in the author's podcast, *Terrible, Thanks for Asking.*

My brother sent me a link to a TikTok account a friend recommended. The woman had lost her husband young. It should have helped. But she had kids. My children are my reason for going on, she said, for getting up and living every day.

But what if you don't have children? What's your reason then?

It was a TikToker from New Zealand named Kelsey Mulcahy who pulled me off the edge. Kelsey lost her fiancé unexpectedly, in an accident while living abroad in England. Six weeks later, she moved to Australia with her best friend. She needed a fresh start. She needed to keep momentum. It was sink or swim. That's how Kelsey said it: You're going to sink unless you swim.

A few months later, she posted about a trip to Africa. She had planned it with her fiancé, but she went with her father. Those pictures, their smiling faces, shifted something in me. Kelsey was my age, she didn't have children, she was finding a way. She was creating a life for herself, doing the things she and her fiancé had meant to do together. Her posts were sad, even after her trip. But as she neared the two-year mark, Kelsey was posting about finding joy. Despite her grief, she was building a beautiful life.

Two years?

Twenty-four months to learn to swim again?

That felt like hope.

I mentioned to Reb the possibility of documenting my journey on TikTok. "You should," she said immediately. "Yeah, Laura, you definitely should." Reb lives online, but not in a bad way.

I wasn't sure it was a good idea. I'm a private person, and I was low, low, low. "It will be good for you, Laura," Reb said. "And that way, we can follow you from here."

I thought about it for a few days, and I realized Reb was right. If I made myself post a TikTok every day, I'd have to leave my hotel every day, or it would be pathetic. I didn't mind sad. I was sad. I didn't want to be pathetic.

I told Reb I'd do it. But I didn't know how. I hadn't posted on Instagram in a year, and I'd only posted one short clip of my dogs on TikTok. I read a tutorial, and even then I didn't know you could take videos inside the app until after my trip.

Before I left, I posted once, as practice. It was a slideshow, photographs of Devon. The post got a couple hundred views. Which felt right. There were a lot more than a hundred people who loved Devon, but less than a hundred people who would follow me.

I was going to post my TikToks privately, for my friends and family. I had my finger hovering over the option. But then I thought of Kelsey Mulcahy, and I thought that maybe my pain could spark a fire in someone the way her pain had sparked a brittle flame in me. So I made it public, and I started with that explanation: "My fiancé died a month before our wedding, and I've gone on our honeymoon alone to see if life is worth living."

Two days later, the post had two million views. It's hard to explain how much that meant to me, not because I was suddenly "famous"—I was not—but because it made me feel less alone. I had a great support network. Everyone rallied around me when

Devon died. My parents. Devon's parents. My brother flew home from Toronto. My sister, Tamara, who was twelve years older and had always looked after me, slept spooned around me every night. Devon's sister, Kathleen, one of the kindest people I have ever known (second only to Devon), stayed for a week and never blamed me for the death of her favorite person in the world, not once.

And yet I felt alone. Like the world was swirling around me, all these colors, all these chattering people, but I was dropping out of it, curling away, recoiling from its touch. Somehow it was the kindness of strangers, the thousands who sent me a message in the hours after that post, and especially the young women who had lost a partner, who saw me because they were dealing with the same isolation and pain, that poked a finger through the rhinoceros armor of my grief.

There were negative comments. People accused me of cashing in on tragedy. Know-it-alls lectured me about gluten. (Really, was that the point?) One girl said I was a fraud, that if I truly loved Devon I wouldn't be on vacation, I'd be home in bed or, even better, dead. That's what she'd do: She'd kill herself if her partner died.

That rubbed Reb, who was back in Newfoundland reading all the comments, the wrong way. Reb tracked down the commenter and told her right where to go. "Block this girl," she demanded after dozens of angry messages back and forth. Which I did. For Reb. Because that girl's comments didn't bother me. She wasn't saying anything I hadn't thought a thousand times.

Most of the comments, though, were positive. People took the time to tell me I was brave, I was inspiring, which struck me as funny, because I was trying to show them what my trip was really like: crying in my hotel room, wandering in a grief-stricken fog, bingeing murder documentaries, eating at McDonald's in my pajamas . . .

What was so brave about that?

DEVON AND I didn't speak much in the office after the kiss. In fact, we barely spoke at all. I didn't want anything to interfere with my job performance, and I still wasn't sure what the firm would think about an office romance.

So I started doing math. The associates and assistants ate lunch in the break room, and both Devon and I wanted to be there, because we loved our coworkers. I made sure to sit near the opposite end of the table—not so far away to be suspicious, but far enough that it made sense to ignore each other. It's a delicate balance. Every day when I walked into the break room, I calculated the perfect distance.

Devon was . . . not as cautious. Instead of "ignoring" me in the break room, he sent me messages. Most were jokes or compliments. Some were NSFW. I'd look up from my phone, and he'd be looking the other way and chuckling, and I knew he was trying to fluster me.

I tried a few risqué replies, but they didn't feel like me. I was too nervous. Our coworkers were sitting right there! I'd have to put down my phone and focus on my lunch.

"Are you going to get that?" my friend Sonya would ask as my phone vibrated with messages from Devon.

"No, I'll check it later."

It was a twenty-minute drive to my rental. I was usually home by five-thirty. Devon arrived ten or fifteen minutes later, and we headed straight to my room.

I can be self-conscious. I have a tendency to question my decisions, especially about new things, and I get uncomfortable when I'm not in control. But Devon made sex and connection easy. He paid attention to everything about me, to all the things I liked and didn't like, to all the signals I didn't know I was giving him. Making me happy. Making me feel . . . free to be myself was what made Devon happy.

I trusted him. That's what was different about Devon: I trusted him completely. It wasn't just sex; there was nothing I couldn't say to him, nothing I didn't think he'd understand. At the lighthouse, he had told me about his deep hurt over the death of his aunt Sue. He had trusted me with his pain before he even knew me. I think that's why I trusted him in return. From the moment we came together, I shared my deepest emotions with him, my most perilous wants. I was never hesitant with Devon. I was never ashamed.

We only had an hour. My roommate, a friend from law school, came home around six-thirty. But that was okay. It's hotter in a pressure cooker.

Afterward, we walked my bernedoodle, Leni. Devon was appalled that I had rented a house in a cookie-cutter suburb on the edge of town. He said I was missing the beauty of the city. As a lifelong Townie—the Newfoundlander term for a resident of St. John's—he felt it was his duty to show it to me. So every day, after our hour in my room, we put Leni in Devon's car and took her for a walk in the city. We explored the cliffside houses of the Battery, the colorful "Jellybean" row houses above the harbor, Bannerman Park, the fort on Signal Hill. Devon showed me his favorite coffee shop, his favorite sandwich shop, a few of the city's famous breweries, though Devon didn't drink. The weather is lousy in St. John's for nine months of the year. They call it RDF: rain, drizzle, fog. So in the summer, every restaurant throws open its patio or porch. The city turns three blocks of Water Street into a pedestrian mall. The restaurants set up tables in the street, and everyone eats and drinks outside.

I promise you, it's not a trick of my memory: That summer, the weather was sunny and 22 degrees (72 Fahrenheit) every day.

On the weekends, we went hiking. I'm a bookish type, but we're outdoor people in Newfoundland. We're surrounded by wilderness; our towns are sparse; there's not much to do besides hiking, fishing, hunting, skiing, boating, snowmobiling, and puttering around your primitive vacation cabin. I hiked the west coast with my family, from Gros Morne to Bottle Cove to L'Anse aux Meadows, where the Vikings established the first European settlement in the Americas a thousand years ago. My mother's house is less than a mile from Marble Mountain. In the winter, it's a ski resort, but the rest of the year it's a two-hour hike with a gorgeous view of the Humber River Valley. I hiked Marble Mountain a hundred times. For me, it was a walk around the neighborhood.

Even in the center of St. John's, the wilderness is only minutes away. The East Coast Trail System, the pride of the Avalon Peninsula, can be entered from numerous points in the urban core and ten minutes later, thirty at the most, you have walked beyond sight of buildings and traffic and other human things. Most of the twenty-five paths in the system hug the coast, with views along the shoreline and over the ocean. The North Atlantic is rugged, the water churning and gray, and the coastline is cut by narrow inlets and rocky gashes, the cliffs fifty feet high or more. But in the summer the cool breeze blows the heat away and the sunshine puts a shimmer on the waves. The high moors are green with short, stiff bushes; yellow with long, stiff grasses; purple and orange with lilacs and other flowers. The trails sweep across the moors into the twisted, wind-ravaged fir trees of the Avalon Forest, then out again to a promontory. Some mornings, we'd drive out to Cape Spear, the easternmost point in North America, and hike the high cold cliffs. Or we'd drive to New Chelsea, where Devon's father had a summer house. Once, we took Leni to the Fort Amherst lighthouse, holding pinkies as she sprinted back and forth across the curving one-lane road, and kissing where we'd spent an hour at dawn.

At least once a week, we walked the staircase cut into the cliffs at the back of Signal Hill. Leni is not a small dog, though Devon nicknamed her Baby Carrot. (I don't know why.) She's sixty-five pounds and energetic. The first time we climbed the stairs, I was terrified she was going to pull me off the cliff into the ocean. But Devon held my hand and laughed. At the top, he pulled me into his arms, and we kissed until Leni started to whimper, anxious to go on. We walked her down the less steep side, past the fort and the highland lake and down into the town.

Sometimes, instead, we'd turn away from the city at the top of Signal Hill and take the three-mile hike across the highlands, past a low inlet, then around the far side of "the Gut," a ramshackle fishing village where the dories lay low in the water. The Gut was once a draining lowland of the city, run-down and moldy, but there's a popular brewery there now, and a public area with picnic tables and food carts up against the water. I liked to stop at the Quidi Vidi Brewery for a beer, brewed with water from passing icebergs hooked by trawlers and pulled into the shore.

And on all those days, on all those walks, we never bumped into a single person from work.

I HAD TO check out of the Hoxton because I had only booked three nights. That was as far into the future as my grief-fogged brain could imagine back in Corner Brook. I figured I'd be on an airplane home by the second day, a wrung-out wreck.

My new hotel, which I booked in a panic from the lobby of the Hoxton, was a shoebox. I posted a TikTok showing how the bed, a single, managed to touch three walls. Not long after the post, the Hoxton invited me back. They gave me a free room, and an upgrade to a suite. Which I posted about, of course.

There was a cost to this; nothing is free. I was spending hours working on my posts. But in these early days, that worked in my favor. I would have spent those hours in my room, scrolling through photographs of Devon, crying, calling my family and friends for comfort. Now, every evening, I had something productive to do.

On the fourth day, for the first time, I even had a plan. I had asked my TikTok followers for tips on London, and they came through with a recommendation that inspired me: a gluten-free doughnut shop. Fortified (deliciously) for an adventure, I headed to Piccadilly Circus, because it was nearby, and it was in the movie *Agent Cody Banks*. Yes, it's a bad movie, but my friends and I loved it as kids.

After that, I went to St. James's Park. I was really hitting the tourist circuit now! A path led out of the park to the corner of Buckingham Palace. I did not go on a tour. I grabbed a seat on a little platform set up for gawking at the silent guards and called Sarah, Devon's mother. She's English. She's lived in Newfoundland since she was a teenager, but she went to university in London. That's one of the reasons Devon and I chose England—and Italy, we'll get there later—for our honeymoon. Devon was always talking, mostly in jest, about "seeing his homeland."

Sarah had been texting me a half dozen times a day, but I didn't have the emotional fortitude to text her back. I'm an odd millennial. I can't just fire off texts. I have to think about them first. So, as Reb constantly complains, I'm terrible at getting back to people. The phone is easier. Sarah and I talked for a good long stretch. She had seen my TikToks. She had downloaded the app to follow me.

After the call, I went to the Waterstones on Piccadilly, the flagship of the famous British bookstore chain. I wandered all six floors. *Why We Die. Never Let Me Go. Brief Answers to the Big Questions. In the Dream House. Yellowface. Babel. Hello Beautiful.*

It was like seeing old friends, like overhearing snippets of familiar conversations. But I knew I couldn't join in. After *The Year of Magical Thinking* and *The Hot Young Widows Club*, I'd tried to read Stephen Hawking's *Brief Answers*. I only made it halfway through. I hadn't read more than ten pages of any book since. But I posted a long video of my trip to the store, highlighting the books I love.

"Oh, I didn't know I was on NerdTok," someone commented back.

Sorry. You're on SadTok. Didn't you know?

THE BIG EVENT in St. John's every summer is the Royal St. John's Regatta. It started as a race between two rowing crews across the harbor and back, but it moved to Quidi Vidi Lake, on the outskirts of the city, in 1828. The day of the race is a holiday from work, so there is a city-wide party the night before. The next morning, thousands crowd the lake to drink and watch the races, when they aren't rained out, that is. Even in summer, the weather in St. John's can be too rough for racing.

A partner at Curtis Dawe lived on the shore of Quidi Vidi, and every year she held an employee party the night before the races. About forty people planned to attend—Curtis Dawe is small compared to firms in bigger cities, but large for Newfoundland. Devon and I figured, with that many friends around, it would be easy to avoid each other.

We did great until the cornhole tournament. There was a random draw among the thirty participants—participation was heavily encouraged (if not technically mandatory)—to make fifteen two-person teams, and of course Devon and I were drawn together.

I remember shaking hands. "Oh, hello, stranger. Care to toss the old beanbag with me?"

The good thing about cornhole is that teammates stand on opposite ends of the court, so I had the best spot in the yard to watch my crush toss bags at a hole in a board. It was pretty hot.

The problem started after we won our first game. I went for a high five. Devon went for a hug. A few more victories—Devon was crushing it, perhaps because he was one of the few sober people at the party—and the hugs were becoming uncomfortably long. I thought, Don't mess up and kiss me, Devon. I had complete faith in myself, even after three drinks, but Devon's a wild card. He enjoys overexuberance.

We made it to the finals, kiss-free. We were up against the two partners we work with the most, so it was interns vs. bosses. We did not take it easy on them. The whole firm was gathered around cheering, and everyone except the other partners was cheering for us.

I played pretty well, just not as well as Devon. He was annoyingly athletic. He was firing beanbag after beanbag straight into the hole. It was all cheers when we were throwing from his end, then mostly groans when we were throwing from mine.

Devon kept calling time-out, coming over to my end, and putting his arm around me for a strategy session. But all he whispered was, "You look really hot, Laura."

"Shut up, Devon."

"I'm serious. You are killing it in that dress."

It was always thrilling when Devon whispered secret, sexy compliments, but the firm was watching. "You're supposed to be helping me, Devon."

"Just throw it on the board."

"What about the hole?"

"Don't worry about the hole. Just hit the board."

We lost. The bosses were high-fiving and pumping their fists, mocking us for our loss. That's what I love about Curtis Dawe, it's the kind of place where everyone feels comfortable losing their cool over cornhole.

Devon gave me a one-armed hug. We were secretly kind of devastated. Both of us hate losing. "That's okay, stranger. We'll get them next year."

After the party, Devon spent the night at my house. It wasn't the first time, but it was still a thrill after all the sneaking around. We laughed about the luck of being paired together.

"I wanted to kiss you," he said, "about a hundred times."

"Oh, I know."

Devon got up early the next morning to go for a jog. He fixed me breakfast in bed. The wind was howling, and it was pouring down rain. The weather couldn't stop Devon's morning run, he was the United States Postal Service of running, but it was too much for a boat race. The regatta was canceled. And when the regatta is canceled, so is the holiday. That's how ten thousand hungover people ended up in the offices of St. John's on the first Wednesday of August.

It was a shame, really. I had been looking forward to spending our day off in and out of bed. But mostly in.

I WAS INVITED to a lot of things by a lot of strangers after my TikTok took off. A lot of men—a shocking amount—offered to buy me a pint. I'm sure they were all nice (sure, sure) but I didn't trust them. The one man who caught my eye was a music promoter who said he'd been following my TikToks with his wife. (Nice touch, mentioning the wife.) He said he'd leave a ticket for me at a small show James Bay was playing that night.

I love James Bay. His music is mostly acoustic, soft and emotional, and I've always been a bit of a "Sad Girl." "Smiling but serious," that's how my mom describes me. "Always thinking." It was Devon, she says, who got me out of my own head. He wasn't a fan of my numerous Sad Girl playlists. He said they were depressing. But then again, he'd never seen me in my Sad Girl years, since he's the one who made it easy for me to smile. That was his magic. Devon made happiness easy. Everyone says the same thing: When Laura was with Devon, she was always laughing. But earlier, and especially during two difficult years in college, it felt like James Bay (and Taylor Swift) was all I listened to.

Now that I was truly sad, I worried his music might destroy me.

I decided to go anyway. For the first time, I put on one of the two nice dresses I'd brought on the trip. *Look at Laura, she's a real adult. Look at Laura, she's totally put together and not falling apart inside.*

The venue was thirty minutes away by Tube, but the ride was much easier than it had seemed the first day, when I was grief-fogged at Heathrow. The neighborhood was sketchier than I expected. The club was down a set of stairs in a basement. It was a legendary venue, the Troubadour, but I didn't know the London music scene. I didn't know that everyone from Bob Dylan (meh) to Adele (oh my god) had played there. I almost didn't go down.

I'm glad I did. The place was small. No, it was tiny. I stood in the back, and it still felt like I was standing right next to James Bay when he walked in front of, maybe, sixty people, and the place was sold out. There wasn't even a stage. James Bay just stood in front of us and played. A little patter, but mostly those familiar chords, those old memories. I cried the whole time, but it was a controlled cry; I could function, even when he premiered a new song, "Hope." Listen to it. Please. It's wistful, it's quiet, but it's strong.

If I fall, if I have to learn to suffer and lose it all, if I have to let it go . . . Still I have a little hope.

A few days later, I received a video message from James Bay admiring my courage, telling me to stay strong.

I know social media can be cruel. It can be harmful. But it can be a place of wonder, too. The kindness of James Bay. Of the Hoxton. Of the thousands who took a minute out of their days to drop me a nice note or recommend a gluten-free doughnut.

It inspired me. It helped me carry on. I still read the comments on my TikToks when I'm low. I still watch that James Bay video message when I need to feel hope. It all still makes me cry, in the best possible way.

I REMEMBER THE first time Devon said the word *love*. We were in his car coming out of the parking garage at the office, so we must have gone to dinner or out for drinks with the other associates, because we never left work together, it would have been too obvious we were a couple. So I was already a little wary, a little uncomfortable, before Devon turned onto Water Street and said, without taking his eyes from the road, "I think I'm falling in love with you."

I should have said it back, because I was in love with him, but he surprised me, and I was overwhelmed by the moment, and I said, "Oh," or maybe nothing at all.

A few weeks later, Devon gave me a framed photograph. He had given me flowers, but this was his first real gift. The photo was by a St. John's photographer known for her iconic prints of the harbor and the city's architectural gems, but this was a close-up of a grubby whitewashed building, taken from across the street. In the center of the white wall, in simple black letters, someone had graffitied:

i love you still.

THE TRUTH ABOUT our relationship came out eventually. It always does. We were at a party with the other associates at someone's apartment. Devon left to drive a few people home. That's him, the designated helper. One of the associates asked how I was getting home. I said Devon was coming back to get me.

She looked at me. I didn't say anything, but I must have smiled.

"Oh my god!"

Next thing I knew, everyone was texting. They texted Devon. They texted one another. Within minutes, everybody knew.

Nobody cared. I mean, they were happy for us. *I should have known,* they said. *Yeah, that makes sense.* They cared that way. But the firm didn't have any concerns. I had been free, the whole time, to relax and embrace the magic. The stress, the complications—that had all been in my head.

MANY WOMEN WHO lost partners reached out to me on TikTok or Messenger. A woman who lost her husband in a plane crash. A woman who unexpectedly, suddenly lost her wife. The woman whose TikTok my brother had recommended in the depth of my grief. My public honesty was helping them, I could tell, in the same way Kelsey Mulcahy's honesty helped me.

I tried to write back, but the volume was overwhelming, and it was stressful figuring out what to say. I knew what these women were going through; I knew how much being understood mattered when you felt alone. Their kindness, after all, was inspiring me. So I thought about every word, and in the end, I probably overthought. The woman who lost her husband in a plane crash, we messaged a few times. It was heartbreaking, knowing I was not the only one. But it was reassuring, knowing I wasn't the only one. I wish I could have had that kind of conversation with everyone, but I didn't have the energy. Sharing my pain with a crowd on the other side of my phone screen: empowering. Sharing intimate messages with a single person in need: powerful but emotionally draining. So if I missed you, I'm sorry. I really am. I know how much being seen matters in the deep, sticky muck of your grief. Almost as much as being left alone and *not* told everything is going to be fine.

I decided I wanted to meet someone like me. Not everyone, just one. I wanted a better meetup than the one I'd had with the grief counselor in Corner Brook. (I'm so sorry. You were lovely. It wasn't your fault, it was mine.) I chose Justine. She was my age, her partner died a few weeks after Devon, and she lived in London. So I messaged back and asked if there was other social media I could use to verify her identity. All I had was her TikTok name. Never trust a TikTok name. She sent me a follow request on Instagram. She was exactly who she said she was. She was suffering, just like me.

She wanted me to come to the suburb where she lived, but the thought of going that far to meet someone I didn't know . . . I couldn't do it. She struggled with the idea of coming into the City. We messaged for a few days, unable to get ourselves together enough to get together.

Those were difficult times. I had my big day in St. James's Park and Buckingham Palace, but then I backslid into crying. This wasn't *Eat Pray Love;* it was *Cry Mope Chicken Wings*. But that's the reality of grief.

On day seven, my last in London, I finally met Justine. She took the Tube to Tottenham Court Road, near my hotel. Her dog came with her. He was a black and gray mutt, a big happy boy with his massive tongue perpetually out of his mouth. Justine never went anywhere without him.

My dogs are my emotional support, too. When I hug Chewy, my eighty-pound bernedoodle, and bury my face in his curly fur, I swear I can feel Devon.

Justine and I wandered around the same three-block area for most of an hour. We trusted each other. We could see each other's hurt. We knew that once we settled in, we were going to have a conversation that was necessary and important, but that we did not want to have. Finally, we went into a coffee shop. Then we went to a park and sat on a bench. Across the way, a little boy was playing with a puppy.

"We were together for a couple years," Justine began. Like Devon and me.

"We moved together to London." Like Devon and I had moved to Corner Brook eight months before he died.

"We were happy. We were in love."

They were on vacation on the continent with another couple

when her partner got out of bed in the middle of the night. She thought nothing of it, figured he was going to the bathroom. Then he stopped, stood at the foot of the bed, and collapsed.

She screamed. She tried to wake him, but he wasn't responsive. When the other couple ran in, they realized he wasn't breathing. They called emergency assistance, but nobody spoke the local language, and they didn't know the address of the Airbnb. Justine had to run into the street to flag down the ambulance. Then the police arrived, and she and her friends were arrested.

She spent the night in the police station. She feared her partner was dead, but nobody would tell her what was happening. No one would confirm the best or the worst. The police released her at sunrise, but instead of taking her back to her rental, a policeman dropped her on the side of a road. She was alone, in shock, in a foreign country.

"His heart stopped," she said. "It just stopped. No one can give me a reason why."

A young father had come to collect the boy and his puppy. They were walking away, the father's hand on the boy's shoulder. The waves were crashing over me, pounding away at the rocks of my heart. It's terrible to be alone, but it's equally terrible to know another human being is living a pain like yours. Here one minute. Gone the next. No little boy, no days in the park, no hand on a young son's shoulder.

I wanted to hug her. Devon, when he was alive, had touched me every day. He kissed my cheek. He rubbed my shoulders. He put his arms around my waist, whispered, "I love you, babeski," in my ear.

You lose that touch when your love dies. You lose the feel of skin on skin. And you crave it. Sometimes you just want to be held.

But I couldn't hold Justine. It was too intimate. So instead, we talked for hours, and it wasn't until we were parting that I hugged her quickly, briefly, and promised to get together with her again. Then we went our separate ways. I was worn out and rubbed raw, nothing more to give. I wandered back to the Hoxton and collapsed into *Emily in Paris,* a show where the main character's problems are refreshingly silly.

But the day was good. Our time together, Justine's story, they were worth the hurt. I had come to Europe and posted to TikTok hoping to meet someone who understood. I found her. And even though I couldn't ease her pain, we saw in each other how hard it is to put your life back together, and how natural and healthy it is to grieve.

DEVON DROVE TO Corner Brook to see me off at the end of the summer. In Newfoundland, there are two types of people: Townies and Baymen. Townies are from St. John's. There's an overpass on the Trans-Canada Highway that signals the end of "town." The Townies have been saying "this side of the overpass" for so long, though, they've forgotten which one they're referring to.

Baymen, at least according to Townies like Devon, are everybody else. In the old days, there weren't roads through the interior of Newfoundland. Everybody lived on the coast, which is craggy, rocky, and sliced up with bays. Baymen were fishermen, mostly, who went inland to hunt and float timber down mighty rivers like the Humber, which empties into the Bay of Islands at Corner Brook. We're a paper mill town. Pop, my mother's father, spent his working life in the paper mill, not on the fishing boats. And yet, he's considered a Bayman.

These days, the Trans-Canada Highway connects the island, and Baymen travel to St. John's. I know people who drive there twice a year for Costco. It's seven hours one-way, so they make a weekend of it, handle their Christmas shopping or their summer lay-in.

Many Townies never leave the Avalon Peninsula, their dog-shaped spit of land dangling off the end of the island. Devon had been away to college. He had been to the Corner Brook area several times to ski at Marble Mountain. He seemed like such a Townie that people at Curtis Dawe joked he'd never been farther than the Delta, a downtown hotel. And yet, he fit right in with my family and friends. Everyone could see it: Devon lit me up.

On the last day of his three-day visit, Devon said he had a surprise for me. I knew where we were going as soon as he drove west out of town, but I didn't say anything. There's only one thing down that road: Bottle Cove.

I had been to Bottle Cove dozens of times, but it was fun to see the Bay of Islands through Devon's eyes. The water is narrow enough to see the other side, where the hills rise stony and cold. The water is gray, churning with waves, the islands brackish green, except for Wee-ball, the round island that sits in the mouth of the bay. The road, hugging the southern coast, rises with the hills, then drops to water level for the fishing villages tucked into the sheltered inlets of the bay. They have concrete docks and cinder-block storage buildings now, but the houses clump tight on small stretches of flat land; Devon loved their determination. He loved the mountain ridges, shot through with waterfalls. He loved the high moor near the end of the road, with its auburn foliage and patches of black water. He loved driving me, listening to Taylor Swift for me, talking with me. That's the thing about Devon, he had an amazing capacity to love the moment.

Bottle Cove is a subtle turnoff, a one-track over a ridge to a small, round inlet. The neck is narrow like a bottle, so the water is calm. Devon stood by the car, his hands on his hips, looking at it in wonder. He smiled his famous "can you believe this is our life" smile. Then he grabbed the picnic basket, and we walked a wooden pathway around the cove. At the end of the pathway, we scrambled up a hill into a forest of short, sturdy firs, real northern survivors, stunted and twisted by the wind off the ocean.

The path comes out on the right edge of the bottleneck. There's a flat plateau, maybe forty feet above the water, close enough for you to feel the thud of the heavy waves hitting the rocks. On the other side of the bottleneck, the land rises into a steep peak, like the Rock of Gibraltar. In front, the Gulf of Saint Lawrence, which separates Newfoundland from the mainland there by at least a hundred miles.

Devon spread a blanket on the grass and unpacked his secret meal. Chopped strawberries. Cantaloupe. Celery. Charcuterie. I knew my sister, Tamara, had helped him, because it was packed in her Tupperware. She probably told him about Bottle Cove, too. But a gesture is in the execution as much as the idea.

We sipped beer and hot tea. We ate our fruits and vegetables. We leaned on each other for warmth, because it was chilly with the wind whipping off the ocean, even in August.

I was going back to Nova Scotia for my last year of law school. Devon was staying at Curtis Dawe. We'd already said we loved each other. Many times. At Bottle Cove, Devon told me it didn't matter how far away I was, it didn't change a thing. He wanted to be with me, not for a summer, but forever.

"No pressure," he said. "But if you ever want me, I will be there."

I'd had many boyfriends. Well, not many, but enough. Some I thought I loved, but they didn't treat me well. Some thought they loved me, but I gently let them down. I tried to date one of my best friends, the nicest guy I knew. I loved him, but I wasn't in love with him.

I never thought I'd find someone like Devon. He had the looks. He had the personality. He was funny. He was *sexy*. And he was kind to me.

I told him I loved him. That I couldn't imagine not loving him. That this was forever for me, too. Then I burrowed into his chest, he wrapped his arms around me, and we watched the sun fall into the sea. Usually, there are six or seven people at Bottle Cove. The sunsets are famous. But that day, Devon and I were the only ones. The sun flares brightest, of course, after it's disappeared. That evening, it set the sky on fire for us.

On my last night in London, I went to *Phantom of the Opera*. I love theater. I've seen *Wicked, Jersey Boys, Les Mis, Matilda, The Lion King*. Not in Newfoundland, of course, but in Toronto and New York. I had planned to see several shows in London, but I couldn't get myself together. I only made it to *Phantom* because an actor in the cast reached out to me on TikTok and left tickets at the box office. It was a beautiful theater: gold scrollwork, a wall of red roses. It was a beautiful show. At intermission, I bought myself an espresso martini, to celebrate my first night on the town since my pajama stroll to McDonald's.

After the show, I met the actor who invited me. He was older than I anticipated. Fifties, maybe sixties.

He was incredibly kind. I can't remember a word he said, but I remember realizing: He knows. He has been through this grief. And he's okay. He made it. When other people said I was courageous for going on my honeymoon alone, I didn't believe them. What did they know? They couldn't see me as I was. They didn't understand. But when this man said it, the words went straight into my heart. They filled me up.

That's the night I began to see myself not just as broken, but capable—and maybe a tiny bit brave.

Nice

I'VE BEEN BEST friends with Rebecca "Reb" Dawson since we met on the first day of kindergarten. Not our kindergarten, our older siblings' kindergarten. We were waiting outside with our mothers. We were three years old. I'm pretty sure Reb approached me. I was a quiet kid. Reb was not.

About five minutes after we met, we were inseparable. We hung out constantly—in school, after school. We dressed alike. I say that's because I dressed like Reb, but Reb thinks it's because she dressed like me. It was probably because we raided each other's closets. We were equals, in other words, but Reb was the strong one. She had my back. I was the girl who got her heart broken and then got mad about it. Reb was the one who dressed down the boys for hurting me. *Scary* was one word our schoolmates used to describe her. *Intimidating* was another. Reb Dawson never took shit from anybody.

We were good kids, but we went through a wild phase together in high school, which I'm not particularly proud of now. (I'm not *not* proud, either. I used to laugh about it with Devon, whose wildest phase was probably blowing off his homework to play basketball.) My parents were divorced. My father was often out of town for work, so I threw parties. Sometimes they got out of hand. Someone kicked a hole in the wall. Someone threw the barbecue grill in the pool. They stole my father's expensive wine. They stole canned moose meat! We had a family dinner one Sunday, and the toilet wasn't working. My uncle found beer cans stuffed in the tank.

Okay, Reb, my enforcer, where were you then?

I went away to college in Halifax, Nova Scotia. Like most of the people at my high school, Reb stayed in Newfoundland. She moved to Halifax when I was in law school, to study to become a dental hygienist. We lived together for two years, and it was like we'd never been apart. She still had my back when boys broke my heart. She was the one who said, about my last boyfriend before Devon: "Look, he's nice. I like him, Laura. But you aren't in love with him."

I broke his heart.

I called Reb after Bottle Cove. She says she knew it right away: Laura's going to marry this guy. She says she heard it in my voice: I was in love.

You know what she heard? Happiness. The easy kind of joy.

After the call, Reb vowed to make Devon her best friend. Not to be best friends with him, but to *make* him her best friend. If he was special to me, then he was special to her. She wasn't going to let him be a casual acquaintance. Of course, Devon loved Reb instantly. They didn't spend much time together, because of the distance, but they texted and FaceTimed. If I didn't answer Reb's texts immediately, which I usually didn't, because as I said, I'm not spontaneous online, I'd hear Devon's phone buzz, and they'd text about me for the next half hour. And when they got together, like at Law Ball, my law school's yearly dance, watch out. Two otherworldly extroverts talking the air out of the room.

The second Reb heard the news about Devon, she booked a flight from Halifax to Corner Brook. She arrived that evening. She came straight to my house from the airport. She . . . enveloped me. She and my big sister, Tamara, slept on either side of me, hugging me in a two-sided embrace.

My father was on vacation in Portugal when Devon died. It took him four flights and two days to get back. I told Reb, "I'm just waiting for my dad. When he gets here, I'm going to go."

"No, you're not," she said. "You're not going anywhere without me."

I was terrible company. Catatonic with grief, then screaming and crying. I stayed in bed for days, wrapped up in Devon's sweatshirt. I put the backpack that held the box that held his ashes on the bed. I hugged it at night when I was trying to sleep, and during the day when I thought I'd die from missing him. My grief was physical, a sharp pain in my abdomen. I couldn't move. I couldn't eat. I was hateful, angry, miserable to be around.

I read an article, I wrote to Devon in the Notes app on my phone. *"Two young lives cut short . . ." And I was jealous.*

> *The one thing no one can answer for me is how I am supposed to go the rest of my life without seeing you.*
>
> *Stephen Hawking thinks there is no afterlife. So I am basically left here to suffer until I turn into dust, too. This can't be all there is for us.*
>
> *Everything feels so meaningless.*

Our other best friend, Janine, came by. She had a six-month-old baby. I couldn't spend time with her because her baby made me sad. What a terrible thing to say, that seeing your best friend's infant daughter filled you with a sadness so crushing you couldn't breathe.

Later, I would read an article that talked about how, when your love dies an "off-time" death, you fall out of sync with your contemporaries. *I was buying a casket,* the author wrote, *during the same summer my best friend was buying a crib.* That hit me hard. Because that distance, that falling away, was so, so real. The summer Janine was nursing her baby, I was burying my fiancé.

And I couldn't face it. I was ashamed of my feelings, but I couldn't help them. That baby, that life, was what I'd lost.

I told you I was terrible. Terrible to be around.

Reb never let me go. Whenever I needed someone, she was there. She bought the biggest set of markers I have ever seen. Hundreds of markers. She bought giant, oversized coloring books. She told me, "Just color, Laura. Just get a marker and color."

I don't know where she got the idea—probably TikTok—but it worked. Even when I was spiraling, the mindless coloring brought me back.

Reb and her fiancé, Kyle, had sold their house in Nova Scotia a few weeks before Devon died. They had purchased a house in Corner Brook, though they hadn't closed on it yet. Devon was going to be their lawyer. They made a nice profit. Halifax real estate was through the roof, and houses in Newfoundland are cheap compared to the off-island world. Reb and Kyle wanted to splurge. Neither had been to Europe. So they each chose three dream European destinations and put those six options in a hat. They pulled the slips out one by one. The last one in the hat was where they would go. It was one of Kyle's choices: Sweden.

"No," Reb said. "We're going to the beach."

Typical Reb.

I was texting with Reb, making plans to spend a few days of our honeymoon on the French Riviera with her and Kyle, on the morning Devon died.

"Come with us," Reb said a few months later, when I started thinking about going on my honeymoon alone.

Without Devon? No.

"Kyle and I will rent a two-bedroom Airbnb. You don't have to tell us now. Make up your mind at any time."

It became a goal. The one thing in my great blank future that I could see. *Make it a week,* I told myself as I lay depressed in my London hotel room, *and you can see your best friend in France. Make it a week, and Reb will take care of you.*

One TikTok comment, early on: "Why would you go to London on your honeymoon?!"

Okay, fair. It rained almost every day. But London was personal to me. It was Devon's choice. And a place like the French Riviera wasn't his style. He didn't really like the beach. That didn't stop him, though, from inviting me to Hawaii to celebrate my graduation from law school.

We had had a few rocky moments over the winter. Relationships are full of starts and stops, little tears and jagged lines, especially when you spend three months together, then nine months mostly apart. But I had been offered an articling position at Curtis Dawe, and I was moving back to St. John's, and we were both excited to slip back into our life together.

We put together the vacation on the cheap. Our bargain airplane tickets meant three layovers each way. For the first week, we used my father's flexible time-share. We were exhausted by the time we got to the resort, especially with the seven-and-a-half-hour time difference, but the room had a view of white sand and blue water from the balcony, and we managed to catch the sunset.

We didn't leave the resort for the entire week, except to shop for groceries. We lounged by the pool. We grilled meat, zucchini, and corn on the cob on the barbecue. We snorkeled above lace coral and sea anemones and schools of colorful fish. We kissed in the surf. We splashed water at each other, then kissed again. We spent most of our time on the beach, where Devon was even more attentive than usual, hopping up from his chair as soon as I needed a fresh drink, more ice, another towel. He was so gracious that I didn't realize for the first few days that he was bored by the beach. I had my books. I could lounge for hours. Devon's podcasts could only keep him entertained so long.

One evening, after a day of lounging, we waded into the ocean. The sun was sitting on the horizon. The water was calm. Most of the other guests were in their rooms or sipping cocktails on the patio. We had the ocean pretty much to ourselves as it began to glow, reflecting the sky, then bloomed with color as the sun disappeared. I looked down and saw dark circles floating in the water. They were turtles, newborn sea turtles. He watched them flapping their tiny flippers, drifting like leaves as they fought the tides. It almost felt as if they weren't moving, as if nothing was moving, but in a minute they had passed us by and disappeared into the deeper water.

The next evening, we came back, and it was all there again: the setting sun, the shining water, the baby turtles. Were they the same turtles? Was the water full of turtles, and we only noticed them in the evening calm? Or were we simply lucky to catch this wonder twice?

I have no idea. I know nothing about turtles. But I remember the joy in Devon's eyes, the look he gave me like, Can you believe it, Laura? Can you believe this is our life?

WHEN DEVON AND I got engaged a year later, Reb took it upon herself to plan my bachelorette party. That's what best friends do, she said. There were ten people on her invite list, and they all had busy lives, especially Janine, whose baby was only a few months old.

I could tell the process was stressing Reb out—she's very type A—and it wasn't worth it for me to see her suffer. Devon and I were getting married in my father's backyard. Reb and Sarah, Devon's mother, were handling the planning. Questions would come up, and Devon would say, "Whatever you want, honeybee," and I'd say, "I don't care, babe," and Sarah or Reb would make the decision. Reb scheduled four appointments for us to look at wedding dresses in Halifax. I bought the first dress at the second store. It was gorgeous, and it was inexpensive. Why did I need to see anything else? Devon and I were so sure of our love, so devoted to spending our lives together, that the ceremony didn't matter. It wasn't going to change anything.

Menus? Flowers? *Color schemes?* All we wanted was for 161 (the last guest count) of our closest friends and family to be with us when our love was officially sanctioned by the government of Newfoundland.

So I said to Reb, "You know what, why don't you and I do something? That's all I want, to hang out with my best friend."

We called off the bachelorette party and planned a weeklong trip to Florida. It was winter, and that's what Canadians do in winter: go somewhere warm.

And we decided to take our best friends, too: our significant others.

This was in April (Canadian winter), three weeks before Devon died. We had seven days through my father's time-share in Fort Lauderdale. There are an ungodly number of drunk American college kids in Fort Lauderdale in April. Our hotel had a blinged-out Taco Bell on the ground floor with thumping club music and flashing club lights. Girls were tottering in high-high heels and chowing down on Crunchwrap Supremes.

Mukbang: two out of ten.

We spent ninety-five percent of our time relaxing at the ocean or the swimming pool. Three out of four of us relaxed there, anyway. Devon couldn't people-watch for that long. "It's thirty-two degrees," he said, "perfect weather for a run." That's ninety degrees Fahrenheit. It was so hot, I could barely hold my book and drink my margarita, and I was under a beach umbrella. Devon ran every afternoon. He was so hot afterward, he spent hours in our air-conditioned hotel room. He wanted me to join him for a nap. That's how he put it. A nice, relaxing afternoon nap.

I told him, "No, I can't, Kyle and Reb are here, I'm going to the pool." But he knew I was a soft sell. I loved afternoon naps as much as he did.

The drunk spring breakers, the heat, the ridiculous Taco Bell: It probably should have been too much. But Reb's enthusiasm and brass made it special. Reb was never going to settle for not having fun.

I remember thinking, The four of us get along so well together. The four of us are going to be traveling together forever.

Four months later, Reb and I walked down to Nice's famous beachfront, the Promenade des Anglais. We stood there in the morning light: Bright blue water. Yachts at anchor. Yellow mansions. Palm trees. Chalk cliffs. A dark, rocky beach. And tourists. So many tourists.

The legendary French Riviera.

I was so uninspired.

Reb had made a reservation at a private beach. The club building was ornate and old-fashioned, with the right amount of crumbling. The beach was packed with vibrant umbrellas in sharp, straight lines. We ordered food and drinks right to our beach chairs. We never had to move, unless we wanted to wade into the water, so I lay back, closed my eyes, and tried to sleep, because I had been in bed for ninety-eight hours over my eight days in London, but only a handful were restful. One of the hardest things to do in the clutches of grief is turn off your mind, which reels through memories. I could see Devon hopping up from a beach sort of like this one for a run.

Devon laughing at Señor Frog's, a tacky beach bar, when the waitress secretly slapped a READY TO MARRY sign on the back of my chair.

Devon cracking open a can of chickpeas and eating them with a spoon. Reb and Kyle arrived in Florida first and texted to ask what he wanted from the grocery store. Devon texted back: *bell peppers and a can of chickpeas.*

I didn't open my book; I knew I wouldn't be able to focus enough to read it. But Reb was in the chair beside me, in her sunglasses and sun hat, and she talked me through those hours, distracting me with a string of stories and thoughts. Filling me in on the latest internet scandal. Showing me funny TikToks to make me laugh.

That evening, we dressed up for a sit-down dinner, my first since leaving home. The meal started badly, when the three of us tried to order drinks in our rudimentary Canadian French. The waitress was not impressed. It spiraled when I tried to explain, in Canadian French, that I was gluten-free. I don't know if the waitress didn't understand the concept or if she hated the concept, but she was spectacularly rude, firing off eye rolls while barking out angry French I couldn't understand.

It was mortifying. Until, as the waitress walked away, Reb glanced at Kyle and started to laugh, and then I started to laugh, and I was out of my embarrassment, out of my discomfort zone, and back in the embrace of my best friend.

WE TOOK THE train to Monaco, with its harbor full of yachts and its mall like a palace, all marble floors and chandeliers. The streets were immaculate; the bushes trimmed; the doorways lined with gold. In Menton, down the coast, the buildings climbed the hill above the harbor, a mosaic of yellow, orange, and umber. The bright colors were reminiscent of St. John's, where the row houses and shops are painted vivid reds, yellows, oranges, and blues to ward off the dark, gray winters. But here the colors reflected the sun and a sea so clear you could see the sunbeams on the bottom, drawing patterns on the sand.

Despite its beauty, I wasn't there. I followed Kyle and Reb, I watched them walking hand in hand, and I lost my way. I drifted into a fog of grief that took me out of time. I snapped back, every now and then, to emptiness and despair. So often in my life, Reb's company had kept me whole, but seeing her with Kyle broke me apart. It wasn't their fault. They included me. They comforted me. They stayed away from triggering acts and conversations. But when they bickered the way couples on vacation do, I thought, Why waste your precious time together on that?

When they discussed renovations to their new house, I thought, Who cares?

Reb wanted to go into the Cartier store to look at jewelry. She never said the words, but I knew she was thinking of wedding rings. And even though Kyle immediately nixed the idea as too expensive, I was already looking at what was intended to be my wedding band and mourning the life I almost had.

We were once like that, I thought, as their hands entwined. I had that once. I loved it. Once.

We visited Menton's famous staircase, the bright yellow Escaliers. I have to tell Devon about this place, I thought.

I took a photo at the top. I have to show Devon this view.

I have to share this thought. I have to share this moment. I have to share that funny bit of conversation I just overheard.

Oh, Devon, you would have loved the Cote d'Azur. You would have loved the water, the colors, the company of good friends. It was always people that mattered most to you.

"It's beautiful, Laura," I could almost hear you whisper when another gorgeous vista took me by surprise and broke my heart. "It's beautiful here. But not as beautiful as you."

AFTER HE DIED, I moved the photograph Devon had given me to the wall beside my bed. It hurt to look at it. It hurt to look at anything associated with Devon, especially in those raw, rough months. But those words, graffitied.

i love you still.

Devon was with me.

i love you still.

Nothing could change what we had.

i love you
still.

Perhaps he knew. Perhaps he understood that *still.* I want to think he knew that I would need a reminder, and yet I don't believe he did. I want to think he's waiting for me somewhere, and yet I know he's not. It's just a quirk of language. But every time I look at that photograph, I still find Devon there.

I feel the comfort of his love.

Reb was excited about my TikTok fame. She was the one who first encouraged me, after all, to post my journey. She had ideas about what I could do next.

Mukbangs, obviously. But also, TravelTok.

TikTok works like this: Someone posts a video that the algorithm picks up and makes viral. That video features a voice-over, a dance move, a graphic image, a line of poetry, a bit of a song. You take that snippet of meme-ability and give it your own spin. You do that every day, because every day something new bubbles up from the algorithmic unconscious, even as something like "I've gone on my honeymoon alone to see if life is still worth living" continues on, chugging along in the background of our collective TikTok conversation. By the time she got to France, Reb had *loads* of ideas for travel TikToks. We had the sand. We had the sun. We had each other. It was, as every single person kept telling me, *an opportunity.*

We didn't film any TikToks together. It was too much work. In London, I spent five hours a day on TikTok: three hours making new posts, two hours reading and trying to respond to comments. I know that's not how social media works. You don't get bogged down in personal interactions. You move fast. You throw content at the wall. But I'm not the kind of person who could ignore the thousands reaching out to me. When I had no energy to respond, the guilt weighed heavy on me.

Laura, I was so sorry to hear about Devon, an ex-boyfriend wrote. I've chatted with a good many people over the last few days, and never has it been so apparent that someone is as unanimously loved as you are. It's very fitting, as well, that someone who never has an unkind word for anyone has, in turn, never had an unkind word spoken about her. I am so beyond sorry.

What was I going to do: Not write back?

Just say "Thanks," and leave it at that?

Pretend that his kindness didn't matter to me? That his message, while unsettling, because people were talking about me, and I don't particularly like being talked about, didn't make me feel less alone?

When I first posted to TikTok, it felt . . . Well, it wasn't fun, exactly, but it was freeing. I didn't worry about the reaction. Only a handful of people were going to see it, and every one of them already loved me. It was an honest unburdening of my soul.

In the days after I went viral, it was exciting. All I had to do was post my honest feelings, and a million people would see me, and they would honor those feelings. For a moment, they would care. Not gonna lie, it felt good. It felt like a release. It felt like, maybe, some people were finally understanding my pain.

By France, it felt like pressure. I had been filming everything.

So many coffees! So many shots of my hotel room! How was I going to sort through it all? How was I going to capture something true about something as enormous as grief in ninety seconds or less? I knew ninety-five percent of the people who viewed my TikToks were just scrolling, but at my numbers, that meant two hundred thousand people were interested in what I had to say. They were invested in my journey. How could I make my daily moments, my little life, feel meaningful to them?

How does one personal journey illuminate something true?

I started second-guessing the video snippets I chose. I started overthinking the message I was trying to convey. Instead of one take for the voice-overs, I did three or four or ten. I edited and re-edited posts for hours, then gave up, stashing them in my drafts.

Reb helped me finish those posts, which were all about London. She didn't appear in them. She wasn't mentioned. So while, at any other time, I would have loved to film some bestie travel TikToks together on the Promenade des Anglais, I hope the many, many times Rebecca Dawson from Corner Brook, Newfoundland, is mentioned in this book will prove how much she means to me. Love you, Reb. You have been with me every step for the last twenty-five years. I couldn't do it without you.

I'M THINKING ABOUT this now, because the drift of these last sections doesn't sit quite right. I'm not comfortable saying anything even slightly negative about Reb, or implying that I didn't enjoy every minute with her after the sacrifice she and Kyle made to be there for me. But the truth is: Reb didn't understand. She didn't know how it felt to lose Devon, and everything his love meant to me, and everything we would have been.

You can sympathize. You can try to put yourself in that position. But you can never think yourself into understanding. It's not a brain thing. It's a heart thing.

And you know what? I am so happy that Reb and I were out of sync. That I was the only one to fall away, that she got to stay the course, to have the life she wanted. I would never want her, or anyone, to feel this kind of pain. And unless you feel it—unless it happens to you—you can never really know.

After Devon died, my parents wouldn't leave my side. My mother, a retired nurse who works at a residential facility for adults with special needs, was able to get a couple months off. She stayed with me during the day. My father, a judge, came after work and stayed with me through the night. They divorced when I was five. I love them equally. But my father was the one I poured my heart out to. We didn't talk. Saying anything, even mundane things, was a struggle in the weeks after Devon died. But every night, I texted him dark thoughts:

Why did this happen?

I'll never be happy again.

I don't want to go on.

Those messages scared my family so much, they took away the knives and scissors. I had to ask my mother for my medication, because she wouldn't leave me with the bottle. My father moved his things to my guest bedroom and lived at my house.

He wanted me to move in with him. He had a four-bedroom outside Corner Brook on the Humber River, with a backyard big enough for a 161-person wedding, so there was plenty of room for a grieving daughter and two dogs.

I wouldn't leave the house. Because it was our house, Devon's and mine. We bought it together. It was where we had planned to make our lives together. It was a square two-story from the 1940s, with enough bedrooms for an office and a nursery. It had a massive, triple-wide fridge. The basement was unfinished and full of spiders; I hated doing laundry down there. The oil heater was old and inefficient. The master bathroom shower leaked, so we showered in the hall bathroom. We'd been there eight months, and we'd barely gotten around to decorating. It was perfect.

I wasn't leaving, even though it was hard to live with Devon around me. His clothes were in the closet. His coat was on the rack by the door. The morning he died, he had gone for a run and left his sweaty shirt and shorts draped over the rim of the tub. I wouldn't let anyone move them. I had been nagging him to hang a hook in our bedroom closet for months. He installed it, finally, on the day before he died.

The nursery . . . We hadn't decorated it, not even with paint. But we always called it the nursery. I had to pass it every time I went out my bedroom door.

So I didn't go out my bedroom door.

Sometimes I came halfway down the stairs, saw my friends and family on the sofa Devon and I had hauled across the island, said "Nope," and turned around.

I'm scared I'm forgetting you, I wrote to Devon on June 10, a month and four days after he died.

And later that night:

> *The dust has started collecting on your glasses on the shelf.*
>
> *Right where you left them.*

How could I leave those glasses, even for an hour? How could I leave Devon behind?

Eventually, my father convinced me to help him walk the dogs. We drove to a park where the path wound along a creek through the woods. The walk was soothing, even if Chewy's playful-puppy personality reminded me of Devon.

I started running. I hated running. But Devon loved running, so I felt compelled by him . . . for him . . . I don't know. It felt like a way to honor him. This wasn't a jog. It was a sprint. I ran until I collapsed, my side splitting, gasping for breath. I fell to my knees and started screaming. When I looked up, my father was there, concerned. Even the dogs were concerned.

I sprinted like that the next day, and the next. It was painful. I was running myself into the ground. But it felt good to have a reason to hurt that badly.

Slowly, over a series of weeks, my mad sprints began to find a steady pace. Devon ran every morning, so running made me feel close to him, even if it was my father jogging at my side. We went surprisingly far, surprisingly fast. Not because I was in shape, I just welcomed the pain. The more I hurt, the closer I felt to Devon, and the farther I wanted to go.

When I decided to go on my honeymoon, my father asked if he could come for a few days.

I said, "Thank you, Dad, yes, please do." Kelsey Mulcahy had gone with her father on her trip to Africa, the one that helped transform her grief.

Unfortunately, the only time my dad could get off work was the week I was in Nice. He rented a room a few blocks from Reb's Airbnb, and he came straight over after dropping off his bags. He gave me a hug. He said he was proud of me. I was thrilled to see him. I love my father. But I couldn't help thinking, as I had on all those evenings he jogged beside me back in Corner Brook: It should be Devon. It would be Devon. Why isn't it Devon?

For a couple of nights, my father and I stayed in, while Reb and Kyle went out for cocktails and an evening stroll. Reb works full-time as a dental hygienist. Kyle works away. There aren't many high-paying jobs in Newfoundland, so men have traditionally worked off the island. At first, it was on fishing boats. By the 1960s, there was a hydroelectric project in Labrador, by the 1980s, oil rigs off the coast. My father's father worked away building and repairing the hydroelectric plant in Labrador. The work was ninety days on, ten days off. Today, many of those who work away go to Alberta, to the oil fields. They say there are more Newfies in Alberta than on the island, that you can't throw a rock in Fort McMurray without hitting someone from home. Kyle was a heavy-duty mechanic for Caterpillar. He worked fourteen days on, fourteen days off assembling and repairing equipment, often in the northern Quebec mines. He and Reb deserved a romantic getaway.

Thank god my father was there. I spent some of my alone time napping, and some of it tinkering with my TikToks, but most of it I spent with Dad. We sat in Reb's Airbnb, or we walked through the old town, talking about Devon. We hadn't talked about him much in Corner Brook. Neither of us was ready then. The most my father would say in Corner Brook was that Devon loved me, he would want me to go on.

I hated that comment. I hated when people told me that Devon would want me to be happy. It's the worst thing you can say to someone in the depths of their grief.

You don't know me like Devon knew me, I wanted to scream. *Devon would never want me to hurt this bad.*

My father loved Devon. Whenever we were in Corner Brook, Devon helped him with his projects. Dad always had projects. There was a huge pile of dirt beside his driveway for what felt like years. Devon helped him finally fill in all the low spots in his yard.

They played crib (cribbage). It was Devon's favorite game. He tried to get me to learn it for years, but I wasn't interested until he started playing it with Dad. I learned it then, because I had FOMO when they were playing without me.

I knew how much losing Devon hurt my father. On Dad's first

night in Nice, he took me to an Irish pub. No matter where George Murphy travels, he finds an Irish pub. We struck up a conversation with a nice Irish couple, who must have wanted a little taste of home. We didn't want to say anything about the reason for our trip, but they kept asking until my father finally blurted, "Laura's fiancé died."

He couldn't say more, he was crying so hard. And when I saw that, I started crying. And then the woman started crying.

"I have three boys your age," she said, wiping away tears.

It's a universal heartbreak: the loss of the young. A death too soon. But I knew my father's trauma was more. He wasn't broken just because of Devon, though he loved him like a son. He was broken because of me. He saw me in pain, and thought it was his job to save me.

But I didn't want to be saved. How do you tell your father that?

How do you tell your father: Quit giving me advice. Stop demanding—not with words, but with your pain and frustration—that I get better. I am not the same. I will never be the same. Just be here for the me that is me now, accept me as I am.

Instead, so often when he looked at me, I saw the strength go out of him. "I can't be anything, Laura," my father told me, "until you're something again."

Reb was in France for the beach and the sun. My father was in France for me. He would have spent a week in a hole, if that's what I needed. His unflinching love was why he was the one I reached for in my darkest moments, why I laid my darkest thoughts on him. He was the strongest, even if every time he held me, I could feel the trembling in his chest.

But I felt . . . terrible, making my father give up his life to live for me. That's the circular firing squad of grief, once you get past the stabbing pain, the wanting to die. I felt guilty to Devon if I didn't think about him every second of the day.

The hardest part about grief, I wrote in Notes, *is the guilt and the feeling that you are forgetting them if you are living your life.*

But it's such a burden, being a burden on your dad.

and yet i love you

every day.

i love you still.

Please don't mistake George Murphy's character because of all these tears. My father is a Bayman. He was born and raised in Cow Head, a fishing village up the western coast. At eight, he and his brother started tearing the jaw meat out of the discarded cod heads behind the local fish-processing plant. They sold these "cod tongues" for a quarter a pound, before realizing they were severely underpaid and raising the price to $1.25. Many people won't eat cod tongues, but my dad loves them battered and fried. He uses cornstarch instead of flour since I'm gluten-free—even though I would never eat a cod tongue. I guess he's holding out hope.

He hunts geese. He snares rabbits in the winter, checking his traps on his snowmobile in the mornings before work, and cooks them in a traditional Newfie stew. He fishes, river and bay. He has three freezers in his garage, filled with things like a fifty-pound halibut, sea-brined lobster, and bakeapples (cloudberries), which he packs in ziplock bags each fall. He "knows a guy" in Blanc-Sablon who can get him almost anything, including seal meat sausage.

Every Newfoundlander is allowed to kill one moose a year, with a permit. Like any good Bayman, my father takes his moose. He gave us a couple packs of moose sausage out of the deep freeze—made by a butcher friend, another "know a guy"—every time we visited him. He gave us moose steaks and moose burgers. George Murphy taught Devon to love moose meat.*

It was interesting to see that man, who loved deep-grilling and deeper snow, on the French Riviera. My father isn't unsophisticated. Far from it. As a boy, he read every book in the Cow Head library. He earned a scholarship to college. It was his first time in St. John's. He put himself through law school in Nova Scotia. He'd been senior partner at a law firm in Corner Brook before becoming a judge. I idolized him. He cared about his clients, and he

* Don't cry, animal lovers. Moose are not native to Newfoundland. In 1878, two moose were released into the wild to provide a cheap source of meat. They promptly disappeared. In 1904, four more moose were released. They also disappeared. But they weren't dead. They were breeding. Today, there are a hundred and twenty-five thousand moose in Newfoundland, and they have no natural predators. If it wasn't for hunters, the moose would overrun the island and destroy the habitat.

cared about justice. I became a lawyer because I wanted to be like him.

We traveled off-island many times: to Florida, Arizona, and California, the warm places Newfies go in the winter. We went to Mexico. We vacationed in Europe. We took a cruise. But George Murphy was a Bayman at heart. We spent much more of our time as kids digging for clams in Cow Head.

He had known Reb as long as I had, and he loved her. (He didn't know about the grill in the pool until last year, that probably helped.) The two of them got along like (sarcastic) daughter and (good-natured) father. On our second-to-last day in Nice, Reb took him to her beach club. My father had been to the beach many times, but never like Reb goes to the beach—all day. It took him six hours to try the water, and even then he tottered toward it slowly, a baby moose finding its legs. In his defense, the beach was rocky at the shore. It took several minutes for Dad to navigate the last ten feet.

It wasn't baby turtles, but I think it was my happiest moment in France, standing waist-deep in the Mediterranean with Reb, laughing at my fumbling, pale-white dad. For five minutes, maybe six, I didn't think about Devon at all.

Le Plongeoir was at the top of Reb's wish list. It's a seafood restaurant built over the sea. You enter through a narrow, three-story stucco building atop an outcropping above the Mediterranean. When I say above, I mean the walls of the building are aligned with the edges of cliffs, which drop straight into the sea. You cross a gangplank to a seating area and bar covering every inch of another outcropping farther out over the water. And then, if you're lucky, you cross a longer gangplank to a covered seating area atop the final rock. Three white platforms stick out from that deck, each ten feet higher than the other. I've seen photos of people diving off them into the sea. There are thousands of photos online, from hundreds of angles, and they don't do the restaurant justice. The place hovers above the Mediterranean. At night, it glows like a lantern above dark water. Even the cliffs are lit up from below.

Le Plongeoir is what Instagram was invented for.

Unfortunately, the entire world has Instagram, so it was booked solid. Fortunately, Reb never takes no for an answer. She kept calling until she got lucky: A reservation opened up.

I put on my nicest fit, a long white dress I'd been saving for such an occasion. I did my hair and makeup, because Reb insisted. This was our—her—big night.

On the walk over, we stopped at an Irish pub. Dad's choice, obviously. Reb doesn't drink beer. She had a frozen virgin strawberry daiquiri. In an Irish pub. In the South of France. In full makeup and her nicest dress.

We caught another break at Le Plongeoir: a table with a view. The sun was setting as we ordered. The sky was a pearly blue. The restaurant shot through with golden light. And then, as our appetizers arrived, the sun fell quietly into the sea, without too many colors, without a fuss.

I felt a sharp pain, like being stabbed. I bent over, then forced myself to straighten. No one had noticed. I felt another pain. It was so sharp, it made me sick. I tried to smile. I tried to stay in the moment with my best friend, her fiancé, my father, in this special place. But when my steak arrived, I pushed it away and headed to the bathroom, hoping to escape before my strange behavior ruined Reb's evening.

They say every seventh ocean wave is larger than the others. They say the seventh wave of the seventh waves can be a monster. This was one of those tsunamis, a wave of grief so large it destroyed everything in its path:

This is a perfect romantic dinner. Devon should have been here.

This is the perfect night. Devon should have been here.

I am wearing my white dress. I am sitting above the ocean. The sun is setting. There is no more honeymoon moment than this moment. These are the moments Devon lived for.

He should have been here.

He would never be here.

I was never going to see the Mediterranean with Devon. I was never going to see Devon, not ever again. Devon, my Dev, was gone.

On our last morning in Nice, I walked to my father's Airbnb. It was a tiny room. "I don't want to go on," I said. "I want to go home."

In Corner Brook, my father's love had smothered me, Reb's kindness made me feel unkind. In France, I had two hearts. One moment, *Please take care of me*. The next, *It is too much*. But the thought of being without them now was terrifying. It felt impossible, this crazy idea of traveling on my own. They were my favorite people in the world. How could I go on without them holding me?

"Go back to London," my father said. "You already have your ticket. If you still want to come home in a few days, I'll pay for it."

I gave him a hug. We took an Uber to the airport. My father flew back to Canada. Reb and Kyle flew back to Canada. I'll see you in a day or two, I thought as I boarded my flight to London, alone again.

London

JUSTINE AND I had been texting while I was in France, so on my first full day back in London, I took the Tube to the suburbs to visit her and her delightful dog. She met me at the station, and we walked along the Thames. The area was nice. Kind of corporate, lots of office buildings, but pristine, quiet, scrubbed. Obviously expensive. It didn't feel like the London I knew. Justine said she liked it because it made her feel safe.

She was moving. Her boyfriend had been paying for their apartment, and she couldn't afford it on her own. His family had arrived unexpectedly and loaded most of their things into a rental van, as if they had belonged only to him. They treated her like his no-value girlfriend, or his negative-value hanger-on, not as a fellow human being who was suffering, who loved their son, who also suffered a catastrophic loss.

I thought about how lucky I was to have Devon's family, as we walked along a gently curving walkway past iron security gates. His mother called me daughter. His sister called me sis. His father texted me every couple days, to see if I was okay. We weren't married, so I wasn't entitled to Devon's death benefits. We had life insurance through our law firm, but neither of us had bothered to do the paperwork and designate a beneficiary, which is ridiculous, because I gave that advice to clients every day: Pay attention to the paperwork, fill it out immediately, don't wait. But who thinks they are going to die at thirty-two?

I knew there was a process to challenge the entitlement to the death benefits, but I told Devon's family I wasn't going to do it. They lost their son. I didn't want to make that even one percent harder for them. They told me, *No, the money belongs to you.*

It wasn't the money that mattered. It was their love.

Justine was clearly hurting. I had lost Devon, and that felt like everything, but Justine had truly lost everything. She had recently moved to the city. She was working from home. She didn't have friends nearby, except her dog, and when she petted him I noticed her hand shaking. She was glamorous, much more than me. Even in grief, she was gorgeous. Would any of the people passing guess that she was scuffling through her last days in an empty apartment, alone, stripped bare? She hoped to stay in the neighborhood, she said, but she wasn't sure she could afford it.

I invited her to come with me to the West End. TodayTix had offered me two free tickets, any show with last-minute seats available. That's what happens when your TikTok goes viral. Companies give you things. Justine was the only person I knew in London, and she needed something nice.

I wanted to go to *Les Mis,* which I loved, but there were some brutal deaths in that show. So I chose *The Book of Mormon,* because I heard it was funny.

It was only after I got back to the Hoxton that I thought, I hope she isn't Mormon.

She wasn't.

I can't say she enjoyed herself. I know her state of mind, I know how distant happiness can be. But she laughed a few times, and I got her out of her empty apartment, and we parted as friends.

And in the depth of your grief, that's all you want: something to take your mind off your loss, a few hours when you feel less alone. Anything more is intrusive. It can feel like pressure. Anything less is falling, infinitely falling.

My TikTok account did nothing for me in France. I'd like to think the French Riviera is above that sort of thing, but they're into the influencer game like everyone else. I simply didn't post about my time in France, so nobody knew I was there. In London, a city I had posted about a dozen times, I had multiple offers for free stuff, from beers with random men (yeah, no thanks) to a river cruise, a hair-and-makeup session, a pottery lesson, a Pilates class. The gluten-free doughnut shop kept offering me free doughnut. The Hoxton gave me discounted rooms. It was odd to see the online universe spilling into the world like that. I'm still not sure I like the way my grief turned into advertising. But in the moment, it was nice. When I walked into the Hoxton, I was recognized. I was welcomed back by name. They made me feel wanted.

One place, the Bicester Village shops, was so aggressively offering me a £500 "Personal Boutique Shopping Experience" that I reached out directly to tell them I wasn't available, I had a train ticket to Oxford. The first day without my father and Reb had been hard. Thank god for Justine's company. By the second day, I was remembering how much it stressed me out to be around other people, because I worried about their feelings. On my own, I remembered, I only had to worry about myself.

The Bicester Village account wrote back, excited: They were practically around the corner from Oxford, in a north London satellite town. They would pay for my train ticket, in addition to my Personal Boutique Shopping Experience. The detour would only take a few hours. Come up in the morning, you'll have the afternoon in Oxford.

I thought, Five hundred pounds. Why not?

Bicester is a charming, traditional English village of crooked streets and tilted pubs set into the rolling countryside near the River Cherwell. The local estate is Blenheim Palace, the ancestral seat of the Duke of Marlborough. It was built between 1705 and 1724; Winston Churchill was born there in 1874. I spent no time in either location, because the area had, for all intents and purposes, been taken over by the Bicester Village shops, an enormous outdoor mall with walking avenues and street signs and quaint wooden storefronts that looked like someone had built a traditional New England village in very old England, then shot it full of steroids until it was twenty-five times its normal size.

I had a nice conversation upon arrival with a young American whose name I can't recall. She was in the PR department. She was the one who lured me here. She handed me my £500 gift card, gave me a few pointers, and left me to my shopping experience. The place was high-end: pavers, awnings, French doors, oak barrels full of flowers. It was like Gwyneth Paltrow's backyard. (Or what I imagine it to be.) The shops were also high-end: Gucci, Dior, Bottega Veneta.

Three hours later, I was back in the PR office.

"How was it?"

"I forgot to take any video," I told her sheepishly. Some influencer I turned out to be. Why had they brought me here, if not to shoot and post video?

Then: "I didn't buy anything, either."

I don't know what I did for those three hours, other than wander into and out of stores. I was in a fog. Sometimes my mind wheeled away to nowhere. Sometimes grief took me to a place and a time, looping through memories and moments. Devon lying beside me on the bed, laughing because I'd never seen *The Fast and the Furious*. (Still haven't.) Devon strapping on his Garmin watch and synching it to his Strava account before heading out for a run. The tiny house we rented in Port Rexton one weekend, where the ceiling in the loft bedroom was so low we were at serious risk of a concussion.

"Let me buy you lunch," the American said.

The lunch was luxurious. Everything at Bicester Village was luxurious. What surprised me was how deep and meaningful our conversation was. When I arrived in England, I wasn't planning to share my story. I hadn't spoken in depth with anyone, even my family and best friends. But after my late-night McDonald's confession, I started being honest with everyone who asked. I had a drink, usually coffee or tea, at the lobby bar in the Hoxton every afternoon. Often, a man chatted me up. They were traveling. They were alone. They were lonely.

They always wanted to know what I was doing in a place like this, ha ha. So I told them the truth: My fiancé died, and I'm trying to figure out how to live again. And you know what? Every one of them instantly became nice. They offered encouragement. They said I was brave, good for me, that's what it took, just going forward, diving in, looking to the future, all the usual words I had once hated, because they all meant moving on. Sure, several gave me bad advice, including an eastern European businessman who advised me to go to Ukraine. But everyone, it was clear, wanted good things for me.

People: It turns out they're pretty great.

The woman at Bicester Village didn't encourage or flatter me; she did something better. She listened. That's what struck me: She was young, my age, but she listened as I poured out my story. She knew the contours already. She had been following my TikToks. But she asked the kinds of questions that got me talking about the details: not just memories of Devon, but my struggles, my emptiness, the stuff too sad for social media. Trying and failing to get out of bed. Curling into a fetal position for so long my muscles cramped. My fear of driving past the place where Devon died. My dread at the thought of going back to being a lawyer, a job I once considered a vital part of who I am. My embarrassment at falling apart during a perfect meal on a perfect night, twenty feet above the Mediterranean Sea.

"It's nice to have a real conversation," she said.

Her job was working with influencers. They breezed in with an attitude and an assistant or three, barely looking at her, just nodding and saying, "yeah," at their phones. She was young, but they were younger. She told me about a twenty-year-old influencer who casually mentioned buying a new apartment in New York City. Her current apartment didn't have the right light for her videos.

She gave me tips on my TikTok life: what kinds of videos to

post, how to market myself, the best ways to cash in. I remember thinking: This is great stuff. I really need to do all this. But I don't remember any of it, and I never followed her advice. I guess it's clear by now that I'm more a book person than a social media personality.

I ended up going back to shopping with new resolve and shooting several scraps of video I never posted. I bought an overpriced sweater—more than three hundred Canadian dollars!—because Taylor Swift owned one just like it. I bought a purse and a matching clutch.

It had been raining on and off all day. By the time I finished, it was pouring. I should have bought an umbrella, but I didn't. I was soaked, and halfway to the train station my shopping bag ripped straight through. My purchases fell into the gutter.

A girl, maybe eighteen, picked up my clutch and walked away. I had to grab my other items and chase after her.

"Look what I found," she said to her boyfriend.

"You didn't find that. I dropped it."

She gave me a look. "No, it was on the ground."

"My bag ripped. You saw it happen. You were standing right next to me."

She eyed me carefully, probably seeing if I'd back down. I guess every person isn't good, only most of them. But she scowled and, eventually, handed back my clutch.

I never made it to Oxford. That's okay. This journey was about what I needed, not what TravelTok told me I wanted. And I was off to Ireland, lovely Ireland, in the morning.

I had accepted, with trepidation, an offer to spend five days in the countryside there—with Devon's mom.

Ireland

When Curtis Dawe offered me a one-year articling position, the prelude to a permanent job, I bought a town house in St. John's. I have always craved stability. In a rush for adulthood, as my mother used to say. I was still in law school in Nova Scotia for another four months, but my brother, Josh, rented the house from me while I was away. He is a dancer and choreographer, burlesque mostly, and the pandemic stalled the business. He needed something cheaper than Toronto.

When I moved to St. John's in May, just after our vacation in Hawaii, Josh moved to the first floor, and Devon moved into the main bedroom with me. This was our first extended time together, or first chance to truly see each other. I knew from our summer together that Devon was neat. He showered twice a day. He wore tailored athleisure wear: pullovers, "performance" sweatpants, tight-cut stretch fabric, that kind of thing. His work suits were by Kit + Ace, his favorite athleisure brand, and he owned two fitted vests. He had six pairs of glasses, although his round, double-bridged specs were his favorite. He was obsessive about his running shoes. He kept them on three shelves in the closet, as if on display. He folded every shirt with the arms tucked in, and every pair of pants along the seam. He even folded his socks. He learned to fold like that while working at his father's store.

After he moved in, I realized he wasn't obsessive about everything. He could be sloppy around the house. If I asked him to clean something up, he would, but he never noticed how the rumpled sheets, half-finished games, and random junk piled up. The previous owner had painted every wall in the house robin's-egg blue. *Every* wall. We were repainting it ourselves, but Devon wasn't committed. He didn't mind leaving a room half painted, with brushes lying around and drop cloths on the floor. And once we adopted Chewy, a second bernedoodle to be best friends with Leni, it was over, as far as cleanliness. Devon and I aren't the kind of people who make their pets stay off the furniture. They're dogs! Why ruin their joy? We're the kind who half-heartedly tell them not to chew holes in the furniture, then cover the holes with blankets. When Devon curled up on the sofa, Chewy would scramble on top of him and lay with his head on Devon's chest. It's one of my best memories, the two of them, content.

Devon had an outgoing personality, as you know, but he wasn't social. He didn't need to be out. He was happy to stay in with me. Most days, after work, we walked the dogs along the coast, or up on Signal Hill, or maybe around the block. Then we hung our jackets, kicked off our shoes, put on a record. A record player was our first purchase together. Fleetwood Mac, Ray Charles, U2, Bon Jovi, Taylor Swift's *Red* (Taylor's version, of course). Devon's sister, Kathleen, gave him Madonna's *Like a Prayer,* because they had listened to it as kids. For weeks, we listened to that record every night.

We cooked together. I wasn't much of a chef, but Devon was worse. He never paid attention to the details. Watching him chop vegetables was a nightmare. He slashed at the carrots and beets. I thought he was going to lose a finger. And the outcome: pieces of every conceivable shape and size. After a few weeks, I sent him off to handle the music while I prepared the meals.

We ate a lot of salads. Stir-fries, too, mostly vegetables and moose. My dad kept us well supplied with moose. We had moose roasts, which I cut into strips. Moose sausages. Ground moose, which I used for a sweet potato shepherd's pie. Chickpea-flour pasta with moose sauce. Devon loved chickpeas. He roasted them in the oven with root vegetables and ate them in a quinoa bowl. That was as fancy as Devon O'Grady got in the kitchen: a roasting pan and a bowl. When I say he ate a head of lettuce for lunch because he was too lazy to make it into salad, it's one hundred percent true. Devon was fastidious about what he ate, but not how he ate it.

He did the dishes, though. That was our deal. And he did them well.

After dinner, Devon watched television, usually while eating a bowl of frozen mangos or berries. He loved NBA basketball so much, he'd watch games from the night before, because it was too early (Newfoundland is an hour and a half ahead of New York City) to watch the games being played that night. I couldn't watch much basketball without getting bored, unless it was March Madness. I read *Tomorrow, and Tomorrow, and Tomorrow.*

Or we played board games and drank tea. I love Scrabble. Devon hated it, because I always won. Devon was notoriously competitive. He kept challenging me, then getting frustrated, then saying he would never play Scrabble with me again. Qwirkle was our favorite, since we were evenly matched. If my brother was around, we'd play Catan, but Josh was rarely around. The pandemic was winding down, and he was back to traveling for work.

At 8:00 P.M. precisely, Devon went to bed. He had a very specific sleeping setup. Two fans on high, pointing directly at him, for air circulation and white noise. An ice-cold room. Devon never turned the heat on in the bedroom—in Newfoundland. A special weighted blanket. (I use it now, I can't sleep without it. It's like a hug.) A $150 eye mask with cups for your eyes, so it barely felt like it was touching your face. (I stole his, so he had to buy another one.) He didn't like the way the eye mask band felt on the back of his head, so he wore a toque and put the band on top of it.

I couldn't go to bed that early. I stayed up to read or watch true-crime documentaries. Even before I was living a tragedy, those documentaries meant a lot to me. Laci Peterson was somebody's daughter. She was somebody's best friend. She was some child's hero. She was somebody, you know?

Devon went to bed early because he woke up at precisely 4:00 A.M. He dressed in his running shoes, his running clothes, his special running watch. He drank a cup of steaming-hot water. Just water. By 4:30, he was on the road for a two-hour run. It didn't matter what the weather was like: rain, hail, fog. It didn't matter what day of the week it was. Devon jogged on the weekend just like during the week. He was committed to his routine.

We weren't hermits. By the time I moved back, Devon had left law to work for the Newfoundland Growlers, our new professional basketball team. This was his second stint in basketball; before Curtis Dawe, he'd worked for our previous professional team, which folded during Covid. He went to every game. We went out once, maybe twice, a week with friends. They knew we always left by 7:30 P.M., though I'm not sure they understood why.

But the constants in our lives, outside of the dogs and each other, were Devon's mother, Sarah, and his sister, Kathleen.

They lived three blocks away, so Devon was always grabbing a snack, picking up something he'd left there, doing small jobs for his mother. Kathleen had a large, energetic dog; we often walked the three puppies together. Sarah and her partner, Randy, did errands for us: picking up our dry cleaning, letting the dogs out if we were stuck at work, fixing the baseboards when Leni chewed them up. Once a week, Sarah had us over for dinner. Afterward, we played Exploding Kittens. Or Scrabble. Sarah was better than Devon at Scrabble, but I usually won.

At the end of my first summer, Devon had surprised me with a homemade pizza party. I remember thinking how special it was that Sarah made me a batch of gluten-free dough. My diet was an inconvenience. Sarah embraced the extra work of me. She took me as I was and welcomed me. She made gluten-free cookies or desserts almost every week.

I loved her. She was good people. She had a big personality, like her son. She liked to laugh, especially with her twin sister, Lucy. She liked to talk. She was never intrusive, just curious. She was like Devon, which makes sense, because she was one of the people who made him that way: She was conscientious. She paid attention. She knew when she was wanted, and when we wanted a quiet night at home. She knew the things we needed and bought them for us before we realized we needed them. I grew up in a family like that. A family that was kind. A family that dropped in on one another, sometimes unannounced. And I missed them. They were seven hours away in Corner Brook. I loved having an unofficial mother around the corner.

Which is why it's hard for me to admit, especially since I know she will be reading this, that I was dreading the prospect of spending five days with her in Ireland.

GRIEF CHANGES EVERYTHING, including your relationships. They become less about the person and more about the way that person bounces off your selfishness, your pain bubble, this new skin between you and the world. It's not you and them anymore, it's you and them and your grief. And of all the people I loved, and all the people who cared about me, Sarah bounced off my grief the hardest. We were, among all of those who loved Devon, the most obviously destroyed.

Her son was gone. Suddenly. Inexplicably. How much must it hurt to lose a child?

But our grief was not the same. I was inward. I wanted to be alone. I'd go quiet for days, trying to piece together the broken splinters of myself. Then I'd break down, as all the pieces I had so ferociously clutched and strangled slid out of my grasp.

Sarah was outward. She wanted to be doing something, anything, to hold on to Devon. She texted me. She called. She flew to Corner Brook the moment she heard, and she stayed two weeks. Within days of Devon's death, she was planning a Celebration of Life. It was her way of keeping from drowning: She was going to plan the perfect memorial. She was desperate to involve me, but I wasn't capable. The thought of the word *memorial* made me physically sick. So I rarely answered her. When I did, it was only to agree. Yes, yes, that's fine, do that, yes, Devon would like it.

Sarah chose a beautiful venue, on a hill overlooking St. John's. It was where the family had celebrated Aunt Sue's life. She hung one thousand photos of Devon on the walls. Literally: one thousand. In the center of the room, she placed three prized possessions: Devon's ashes, in a box inside his backpack. Devon's favorite basketball. And the backpack I was wearing the day I climbed twelve floors for my interview at Curtis Dawe. The reason Devon called me "Backpack Girl."

Time, the heart: If I'd been able to think, I would have brought the photograph Devon took of our first sunrise. At times like this, the memories, the moments, they're all we've got.

I wore my wedding shoes. Instead of black, I wore a flowery dress. We arrived a half hour early, so I would be there first. But people were already there.

The first person I saw was Romy, a childhood friend who lived in England. She had come straight from the airport. I held on to her and cried.

When I finally let go, the room was packed. Staff from Curtis Dawe and Poole Althouse, the law firm we were working at in Corner Brook when Devon died. Devon's friends from school. Teammates he'd played basketball with, and kids he'd coached in the local league. His family. His family's friends. Our neighbors. Within a week, Devon was friends with all our neighbors. After eight months, I barely knew their names. Even some of Devon's elementary school teachers came. The line of cars was so long, someone said, it took half an hour to get into the parking lot.

I saw so many people I knew. I saw so many people. I couldn't believe how many Devon knew. I saw a group from Curtis Dawe, people I loved, and I wanted to apologize for betraying them, for leaving after all they'd done for me.

I wanted to scream, Why did I do it? What have I done? We were so happy in St. John's. We were happy. It's all my fault!

Then Devon's Aunt Mary, his grandmother's sister, collapsed. She was talking with my mother, in the middle of the crowd, when she reached out and grabbed Mom's shoulder. "I don't feel well," she said.

She slumped to the ground.

My sister, Tamara, rushed me away when Mary fell. A partner from Poole Althouse put his coat around my shoulders. But I'd seen it. Mary was standing right in front of me when she had an aneurysm, and I knew she was dead. Tamara was worried I might lose it, that the tragedy might snap me. It almost did. I felt myself blacking out.

But I didn't yell. I couldn't cry. I was in shock. The three days I was in St. John's for Devon's Celebration of Life, I was in shock. These snippets, these faces, they're all I remember. I gave a speech a few hours after Mary died. I have a copy, because I wrote it down ahead of time. I don't remember giving it. By then, I had gone inside myself, curling around the ember of love still burning there, the last light in my life.

It was Sarah whose feelings were ragged, whose nerve endings frayed. Her row house was full of Devon: a collage of photos, a full refrigerator door. She insisted I stay with her every time I came to St. John's, in Devon's old bedroom, with the things he'd left behind.

I couldn't tell her how painful that was: to lie alone in Devon's bed. I didn't want to be there. I didn't want to be anywhere else.

Sarah needed me to be her daughter. She needed to draw me close, because I was there in the collage; there on her refrigerator; I was the primary thing her son had loved and left behind. She needed me, and I wasn't able to give her what she needed. No one could. No one could bring Devon back. And that's what made it so painful to be with her.

"Tell me," she said one afternoon in Corner Brook, in the house Devon and I had shared. This was a few weeks after Devon died. "Tell me what he said at the end. Tell me you told him you loved him."

She knew immediately she had made a mistake. I saw the shock just before she rushed out of the room. "I ruined it," she said later. "I ruined it all."

I barely noticed her leaving. I was already curling away.

Because I didn't tell Devon I loved him. The truth of that tore through me like a saw. Devon died in my arms, and I didn't tell him I loved him. I didn't comfort him. I didn't tell him how much he meant to me. He was terrified. I saw it in his eyes.

And all I said was, "Breathe, Devon, breathe. You're going to be okay."

I WAS OVERWHELMED when I stepped off the plane in Dublin, but overwhelmed was my default setting on my solo honeymoon. Every morning, I thought, *How did I end up here? What was I thinking?* Of course I said yes when Sarah asked if I wanted to meet her in Ireland. But I never thought I'd be here. I was three weeks into my honeymoon alone. I never thought I'd make three days.

I was afraid. Of losing my resolve. Of collapsing into anguish at the sight of Devon's mother. Of feeling a pain too hard and true to bear.

And yet, I was relieved when I saw Sarah and her twin sister, Lucy, sitting in the airport terminal, drinking coffee. They weren't looking my way, but somehow, I felt Sarah's love, this wave of warmth that washed right over me, and I knew I was back in caring hands. Then she noticed me. She smiled and waved. She glanced down, and her lips clenched, a reaction I knew well: a shot of pain. My suitcase was her bridal shower gift. Devon had chosen the color.

We hugged, the usual pleasantries, and then, *How are you really, though? You look great. You, too. Are you okay?*

We didn't have an answer. At least not one simple enough to share in an airport. So we headed for the rental car. It was a silver Toyota Yaris, which is about half a car. It never would have passed for adequate in Newfoundland winters. I'm not sure it was big enough for snow tires.

"The agent tried to upsell me on a bigger model," Lucy complained. "They always do that at these places."

I thought, I would have paid the difference.

The Yaris was so tiny, I barely fit in the back seat. My legs were torqued sideways, and my head was touching the ceiling. I'm five foot three. I had given my second suitcase to my father to take home after France. Travel by plane in Europe is cheap and easy if you only have a carry-on. My one small bag wouldn't fit in the

Yaris's trunk with Sarah's and Lucy's carry-ons, so I had to hold it on my lap. We weren't ten feet down the road before the car started bucking and stalling, jerking forward, lurching to a stop. It was a stick shift. Apparently, Lucy only *allegedly* knew how to drive stick.

"Work the clutch," Sarah said.

"I know, I know."

"Push down on the pedal."

"I know!"

At the first turn, Lucy had to jerk the wheel to avoid an accident. Not for the last time. Multiple larger and better-driven cars were forced to the curb by that wild, impetuous Yaris. Lucy was so focused on getting the gears right, she kept forgetting the Irish drive on the wrong side of the road.

By the time we hit the countryside, Sarah and Lucy were bickering. They're British, but they grew up on a farm in Africa and moved to Canada as teenagers, so no, they don't sound like *The Crown*. They had lived in St. John's, within a few miles of each other, for forty years. No sisters could be closer, or love each other more, which meant they contradicted each other constantly and challenged each other about everything.

In this instance, it was Sarah's inability to read the map. Not the GPS, the map. Sarah had brought an atlas, so she was flipping pages and pointing at lines on paper, trying to figure out where we were. We must have taken ten last-second turns, and each time, halfway through, Lucy would suddenly remember that *everyone is driving on the wrong side of the road*.

At least half those turns, by the way, were wrong.

It should have been hilarious. Sarah and Lucy are energetic and fun. Even now, I'm laughing with them, with love, with so much love.

Unfortunately, I'm prone to carsickness. I was scrunched in the back seat, tossing from side to side, barely hanging onto my airplane breakfast. I had the route on Google Maps, and I was trying to subtly—and then not so subtly—guide them onto the right roads, but they couldn't hear me over the bickering. Eventually, I gave in, closed my eyes, and let fate take the wheel. The drive was supposed to take an hour, but that only brought us to a gas station in the Irish countryside. Sarah went in to ask directions and came back with another map. The last twenty minutes was a two-lane track. Sheep pastures, mostly, but Lucy managed to drive into every bush.

Finally, we topped a ridge, and there it was below us, spread out in the golden light that follows a day of rain: a whitewashed farmhouse with a thatched roof, a green pasture sloping down to a distant sea, and a rainbow in the sky. That's not a metaphor. There was a rainbow, so bright and defined it touched the ground. I don't think it was a sign from Devon or anything like that. Or maybe it was. Either way, it was beautiful.

I stood out in the field by myself and let my mind go blank as I watched the rainbow fade, then scatter, then disappear. Even after it was gone, I stood there, looking out at the sea, remembering our picnic at Bottle Cove, and the way Devon held me close against the cold. There was no rush. I had plenty of time. It took Sarah and Lucy fifteen minutes to figure out how to open the house's electronic lock.

THE PLACE I most associate with our summers in St. John's is Aunt Lucy and Uncle Jim's cabin. It was a small ranch house fronting a huge deck overlooking a narrow valley, with the North River sparkling to the left, a marshland full of vibrant yellows and reds to the right, and a mountain rising directly across the river. North River was where I met Devon's extended family. His niece Bailey was turning seven, and she was having a dog party, so we brought Leni. I was shocked by how many people were there. At least thirty, almost all family, with at least ten dogs. But Bailey ran right to me as soon as we arrived. She started asking me questions about who I was, what I did, that kind of thing. They weren't suspicious questions; they were enthusiastic. Bailey idolized Devon. She thought he was the coolest. If Devon liked me, she figured I must be the coolest, too.

Devon and I went to North River five times our second summer in St. John's, maybe more. It was an open invitation, and people gathered there: Lucy; Jim; their children, Daniel (Bailey's father) and Jamie; Devon's four brothers, as he called them, though they were actually his cousins, Aunt Sue's four boys. The youngest moved to Los Angeles, but the other three lived in St. John's. Brett and Scott, the closest to Devon in age, were, except for a few incidents and growing pains, his lifelong best friends. The brothers shared a weekend place a few miles away, Snow's

Pond, which they inherited when their mother died, but they spent much of their time at Uncle Jim's.

The boys had been, since childhood, a rowdy bunch. Uncle Jim and his friends had started a tradition back in the day. When someone got engaged, they put him in a rough casket they had hammered together from scraps and carried him to all the bars on George Street, a two-block alley in St. John's reputed to have the highest concentration of bars in North America. They put the casket on the bar, with the victim inside, and made him drink until he couldn't speak.

Devon's generation put their own twist on the tradition. When Sue's oldest got engaged, they took Uncle Jim's casket across the river and hauled him up the mountain. Well, a little way up the mountain. The coffin was too heavy with the victim inside. But at the top, they made him get in and pushed him bobsled-style. It was summer, no snow. The thing never went far before grinding to a halt in the dirt. Still, they managed to smash it against a tree. They carried it the rest of the way down.

"Morons," Jim scoffed, shaking his head, but anyone could see he adored his nephews.

The boys were more subdued by the time I came along. Life mellowed them, I suppose. Scott, the second oldest, had gotten married in an impromptu ceremony when he found out his mother's cancer was terminal, so there was no time or appetite for casket jokes. Devon was the best man. But when Sue was dying a few weeks later, Devon was not allowed to see her. She was too sick for non-immediate-family visitors.

It was only Sue insisting, "Where is Devon, I want to see

Devon," that allowed him to kneel at her side and tell her how much she meant to him.

Time. It's precious. So precious.

Sadness wasn't the prevailing mood at North River, though. The prevailing mood was joy. We came with Leni and walked her along the river. We swam. We grilled. We had bonfires and played charades. We ran around the backyard, wrangling nieces and nephews. Eventually, Devon, Scott, and Brett would tire me out—the brothers shared Devon's golden retriever energy, even if they weren't quite at his level—and I'd retreat to the deck, which was splintery, unstained, and perfect. Jamie, Kathleen, Aunt Lucy, and Sarah were usually up there, having drinks with Uncle Jim.

"Welcome to the party, Laura," they'd say. "What'll you have?"

SARAH AND LUCY were "Glitter Girls," a group of fourteen lifelong friends (thirteen after Sue died), who went dining, dancing, and traveling together in glittery pantsuits and dresses. The Glitter Girls had come several years before to the farmhouse in Carlingford, County Louth, Ireland, which was owned by a friend of Lucy's, so of course it was top rate. The Glitter Girls did not do ramshackle. The Carlingford farmhouse had been modernized with double-pane windows, a new kitchen, and whitewashed walls. The barn was converted into bedrooms. We didn't use it, but Sarah and Lucy stayed there when the Glitter Girls descended on the area. That must have been a hoot. The Glitter Girls did not do quiet and subtle, either.

Unfortunately, since the house often sat empty, the spiders had moved in. They say spiders are everywhere, that a human being is never more than six feet away from a spider, which . . . does that mean airplanes, too? Are airplanes full of spiders?

The daddy longlegs on the toilet paper, when I casually reached over to pull a few squares off the roll, that was eight legs too far.

Other than the spiders, though, the house was lovely. It was comfy, quiet. Relaxing. London demanded you get up, get going, do something. In Nice, thanks to Reb's enthusiasm, there was always more to see. In Ireland, the world said: Take your time. Don't hurry. Watch the sheep eat grass. Stare at this rainbow. Don't worry about the hour you spent crying. Don't worry about getting better, whatever better means. Sit on the cliff at sunrise. Take out the heart memento. Picture the lighthouse. There's time.

MY CHILDHOOD FRIEND Janine—the one who two years later would be nursing her baby while I mourned Devon—got married during my second summer with Devon. The wedding was outside Corner Brook, halfway to Bottle Cove. As a kid, I had been friends with the two kids who'd lived in the house before it became an event space. I spent several weekends there. The house was grand, especially for those days, and the backyard was gorgeous. It was on a bluff high above the Bay of Islands, with a view for miles.

Janine's husband was a real Bayman: a professional fisherman, like the generations before him. This was a true western Newfoundland wedding: in communion with the water, elegant in its simplicity.

I went over alone a few days early. Devon had to work a Growlers game. I told him he didn't have to come, but he insisted. He finished work and started driving at 10:00 P.M. He arrived at Dad's house just after 5:00 A.M. and slept for a few hours, then drove me to the wedding. He danced with me at the reception, helped us clean up after the last guests left, then jumped back in his car and drove back across the island, because he had work the next day.

"You didn't have to do that for me," I told him. "I know you love me."

"I didn't do it for you," Devon said. "I did it for Janine."

He was maybe the fifty-seventh most important person at that wedding—maybe—but Devon wanted to be there because he wanted Janine to know he cared about her.

A few weeks later, we went to the wedding of one of Devon's friends from college in Ontario. It was pretty high end, like it was destined for Pinterest. That's not an insult. The whole weekend was picture worthy.

It was at that wedding that Devon and I started talking about getting married. It wasn't awkward or anxiety-inducing. The idea just slipped into the easy happiness of our time together, as natural as discussing whether we were going to have stir-fry again for dinner, or whether it was time for something else.

Our conversation wasn't, Are we going to do this? It was, When are we going to do this?

It was a sign of our comfort with each other. An outgrowth of our trust. It was our inherent understanding that we wanted to keep our relationship simple, and keep our wedding Newfie.

ON THE SECOND day in Ireland, we woke up late and ate a leisurely breakfast. Then we hiked the hill behind the Carlingford house. What looked like a trail turned out to be sheep paths. They split in a dozen directions, only for half of them to disappear and the other half to come back together a hundred yards ahead. Sheep are amblers. All they're looking for is grass.

Sarah was frazzled. The Glitter Girls had climbed this hill; she kept insisting she knew the way. She would walk a ways in one direction, then double back and follow a different branch. That wasn't like her. Sarah plunged into things. She could get in over her head, but she wasn't flighty. She didn't get nervous and argumentative. But she kept insisting something was wrong, this wasn't the way.

I kept walking. The East Coast Trail System was like this. It wandered through highlands and splintered over hills. Devon and I never worried about where we were going. We let momentum take us. Once, we found ourselves skidding down into a hidden cove. The trail was steep, and I worried we were lost, but in the deep water beyond the mouth of the cove was a pod of whales. They must have been feeding, because they kept diving under and breaching out of the water. Devon waded out from the shore, watching the giants splash two hundred yards away, the feel of their bodies hitting the water rumbling like gentle thunder. Leni wandered into the water barking, not that the whales paid any attention. Devon turned to look at me.

"Come here," he said. "Come out with me."

"I'm fine right here," I said, because what view could be better than Leni, Devon, and a pod of whales.

There were no whales over the hill in Ireland. No cliffs or dangerous outcroppings. There was no danger at all. The only thing you had to do was keep going up, and you'd make it to the top.

The view was green up there. Exceptionally green.

The next morning, Sarah slept in. She wasn't feeling well, Lucy told me, and I knew what that meant. She'd probably been crying all night. So I took a walk alone, while Lucy looked after her sister. If I had to pinpoint one thing that smoothed my time in Ireland, that allowed Sarah and me to share our grief without breaking, it was Lucy. She loved her sister fiercely, and she understood her needs. She engulfed Sarah with love.

We can't live life alone. We need to be alone sometimes, but not all the time. Not at our lowest. And that makes loss hard, because there's some love that cannot be replaced. I've cried through so many nights, feeling the truth of that in my bones.

But it passes. Remember that: It passes. By lunchtime, Sarah was strong enough to take the train to Dublin. (We learned our lesson about Lucy's driving.) We went to Grafton Street. We walked through Temple Bar. I went to a bookstore to buy a Claire Keegan novel. We paused at the famous statue of the cockle seller whose boobs are inappropriately large. The metal is shiny from all the people who fondle them.

In the evening, we strolled from our farmhouse down the one-lane track to Carlingford, a picturesque mix of white-painted bars and red-painted shops. At one end was a ruined castle from the twelfth century; at the other, a park with leprechauns, unicorns, a fairy village, and a giant novelty chair. In the center was the Ma Bakers pub, where Sarah and Lucy drank beer while I sipped a cider. The town is little more than a few streets along the lough—Irish for an inlet of the sea—but Sarah made me take a photo of the map outside the village center for consultation. I saw no need to tell her Google Maps was good for walking, too, and it was always on our phones.

Take your time. Sip your cider. Picture the sunrise. Love each other. Be there for each other. Relax. Breathe, Laura, breathe. It's going to be okay.

Sarah was thrilled about my TikToks. This was a woman who loved paper maps. Who brought three guidebooks to Ireland, with pages marked and passages underlined. Who gave me a guidebook for London when I decided to go on my honeymoon alone. Who grabbed the pamphlets at every store. Who kept her texts on maximum zoom, so large you could read them over her shoulder from three rooms away.

"Of course you went viral," she said. "You're Laura Murphy."

No, come to think of it, Sarah didn't say that. It was Devon who would have said that, one hundred percent.

But Sarah didn't seem to grasp how odd and rare this phenomenon was. I didn't fully understand it, either. Somehow I'd lucked into striking the right chord, saying the right thing, finding the right tone. And I wasn't entirely sure that was a good thing.

Sure, some people said I was disgusting for using a tragedy to chase clout. So what? I didn't care about clout. I never doubted my motives.

They said I was ungrateful for moping my way through a nice vacation. So what? If I had been home rotting away in bed, they'd have hated me for that, too.

They even made fun of my tears.

I didn't care, because I'd lost the only thing that mattered to me, so all their insults felt bitter and small. But also, because Devon taught me not to care. He bit into raw green peppers like apples. He ate frozen mango out of a fluted bowl with a special, tiny spoon. He drank a gray protein-powder smoothie every morning, then brought the mixer to work so he could keep filling it with water and drink every last bit. It was disgusting. Devon was odd! He was so brilliantly, lovingly odd.

He had taught himself to be himself, to not worry what others thought.

There was a law partner who didn't like Devon for his chitchat and nicknames, his constant cheerful attitude. It bothered me how condescending the man could be to him. I know Devon noticed. He was perceptive. But he never acknowledged it. He never let it get him down. And he never changed. I learned to trust myself, and be secure in who I was, from him.

But the fact is, I'm a private person, and I was sharing painful, intimate feelings with millions of people on social media. I never intended to do that. And sometimes it felt like a betrayal. That pain, that sadness, it should have been kept between Devon and me.

It should have been ours, and ours alone.

"Devon would have been proud of you for your TikToks," Sarah said. It was the first time we had really talked about Devon, though he was always between us. When Sarah was frazzled on the hill, when she was quiet on the train to Dublin, when she argued with the sister she adored, the loss of her son was at the center of it.

"Devon would be happy for you," Sarah said. "He would be happy this trip happened."

And even though I had always hated when people told me what Devon would have said and felt, I believed her. The only thing Devon ever wanted for me was everything.

I hadn't posted since the London videos I finished with Reb in France. Every day I told myself I should, that I owed my followers something. That's the danger of TikTok's incessant churn: It feels like whatever you're doing, it's not enough. But I didn't want to post, because I didn't feel I had anything to say.

Until, one afternoon, I started flipping through the photos of Devon on my phone. I did this often. I got lost in his face so many times. Almost every photo was a memory, and that was hard. The ones that didn't conjure memories, that I couldn't contextualize in time or place, those were heartbreaking.

I spent hours with Devon that afternoon. Reliving moments. Smiling through my tears. And then I realized, suddenly, that I hadn't posted about Devon since my first post back in Corner Brook. All the TikToks of my travels had been about me.

I made a slideshow of photographs of Devon, set to the Taylor Swift song "loml" (that's Love of My Life, non-Swifties). On the first slide I wrote: "You are so much more than this sad thing that happened to you and I want people to know that."

I pinned the post to the top of my TikTok page. Immediately, it was heart, heart, heart, heart, heart. By the next morning, the photos of Devon had been viewed a million times.

I THINK IT was my third day in Ireland when I had my interview. From the moment my first TikTok went viral, I had been turning down media requests. The *Today* show reached out. *CBC News* wanted to interview me. I wasn't ready. I said no.

That didn't keep me off the internet. It meant people wrote about me without my input. *People,* for instance, wrote a story about my trip, accompanied by a stock photo of a businesswoman walking through an airport. That got picked up by other sites and rewritten, which meant that before long I was everywhere, but almost nothing being written about me was true.

One site blasted the headline: "Would You Go on Your Honeymoon If Your Fiancé Died?"

They had commodified and quizzified my pain.

I decided to say yes to *The Washington Post* because it was a reputable paper, and (at the time) my father read it every morning. I sat again in the main room of the farmhouse, looking out that huge back window over green Irish fields, over intermittent sheep and ancient rock walls, and across the water of the Carlingford Lough, and thought about all the things I wanted to tell the world about Devon. I'm not witty, although Reb apparently described me that way. They interviewed her, too. I'm not quick on my feet. I studied before meetings and court appearances, trying to anticipate questions and think through my answers. It calmed me. Hard work was the secret of my success.

But this time, for some reason, I wasn't nervous. The worst that could happen: It had already happened. Nothing this woman might write could come close.

The first question she asked me: "Have you always been funny?"

Funny? I'm not funny, I'm heartbroken. I think my answer was *no*.

"How did it go?" Sarah asked. She was excited. I was relieved, because it felt like a real conversation. I had talked about Devon. I had taken the opportunity to share the burden, for thirty minutes, of so many heavy things. I was sure of that. And yet, I couldn't remember a single word I'd said.

"She was nice," I said.

"Okay, but how did it go?"

"I don't know. But she was nice."

THE MOST MAGICAL place in Devon's life wasn't North River, it was his cousins' place, Snow's Pond. I heard about it all the time:

Snow's Pond, Snow's Pond, Snow's Pond. In the 1970s, Uncle Jim's father had bought a cabin with no running water or electricity in a forest on the edge of a lake forty miles from St. John's. There were only twelve cabins scattered around the lake, so the place was serene. Over the years, the cabin had been updated and expanded. Eventually, it was inherited by Uncle Jim and his siblings. Before he bought his North River property a few miles away, it had been the epicenter of the family's life.

Every summer of his childhood, Devon spent ten weeks at Snow's Pond. Uncle Jim, a successful artist, and Aunt Lucy spent their summers at the cabin, and since Sarah was a school speech pathologist with summers off, she spent long weeks up there helping watch the six or eight or ten cousins who came in and out as their schedules allowed. It was a summer of formless adventure, as the children spent their days running through the woods and playing in the lake, as they got in arguments and competed in made-up contests, with just enough adult supervision to make sure no one was maimed. At night, they roasted sausages over the fire, and Uncle Jim brought out his guitar.

By the time Devon was eight or nine, the family had a tradition of ending each summer with what they called "the Big Weekend," a themed, game-based Saturday with a talent show at night. All the kids took the talent show seriously; they worked on their songs and skits for days. When he was eleven, Devon and his cousin Scott decided to be the emcees. They spent a week coming up with comedy routines based on things that had happened over the summer. They designed costume changes. They made up songs. Their act was such a hit that, by the time they came on stage, the adults were chanting for more, and Scott and Devon had decided they'd be emcees not just the following year, but every year, forever.

That was a hard time for Devon. As they entered middle school, many in his friend group moved on to "cooler" friends, and he was hurt and lonely. What made him so wonderfully Devon—his cheerfulness, his talkativeness, his unapologetic oddness—made him a schoolyard outcast. His safe place became Snow's Pond, and Scott became not only his fellow emcee, but his best friend and partner in, if not exactly crime, then foolishness.

One summer, they took apart a perfectly good rock wall to "improve" it, but couldn't figure out how to put it back together. Uncle Jim wasn't happy. "Smash and Dash," he called them.

Another year, Devon found a can of red spray paint. He and Scott sprayed R + R, for their (self-given) nickname, Rock 'n' Roll, on everything they had improved over the summer, including a bedroom wall. So not only was everything broken, it was defaced.

That was Devon. He was not handy. But he was confident he could help. If he saw a problem, he tried to fix it. Jim begged him not to, and then Sue begged him not to after Jim bought North River and passed Snow's Pond to her, but in the end, they forgave him his destruction. Devon had a lifetime free pass, Jim said, because he had worked with him for weeks on a project while all the other kids worked a few hours and buggered off. That was Devon. He kept his word. Twenty years later, Jim couldn't remember the project, but he thought it was the stage they built for the annual talent show.

The rock wall and spray paint weren't Scott's and Devon's only terrible ideas. They bought a blow-up baby pool from Walmart and made a hot tub on top of Signal Hill by lugging boiling water half a mile from Aunt Sue's house. It was -12 degrees (10 Fahrenheit). They had to shovel snow into the pool to cool the boiling water.

"The easternmost hot tub in North America!" they declared as they lounged in a fog so thick they couldn't see the lights of St. John's a hundred feet below.

One morning, they spotted a hideous La-Z-Boy recliner on the side of the road. It was perfect for Scott's basement. But Aunt Sheri, Uncle Jim's sister-in-law, wouldn't let them bring it into the house, no matter how many times the boys insisted that they needed a second chair for playing video games. It wasn't even her house! So they loaded the La-Z-Boy into Scott's truck—Scott was sixteen or seventeen by then—and dumped it in Aunt Sheri's front yard.

They took photos to taunt her. But it wasn't quite . . . satisfying enough.

So they put the La-Z-Boy back in the truck and drove it to Snow's Pond. They dragged it across the yard. They loaded it onto a canoe. It was too wide. It hung off both sides. But Devon had the bright idea to lift the footrest and lean the seat flat. "For balance." Then he stuck his leg over the edge of the canoe—for balance—and they rowed the chair across the lake.

On the other side was a hill with a flagpole on top. They called it "Underwear Hill." One summer, the boys had rowed over, only to realize they had forgotten the flag. So they made Drew Mac, the youngest, strip down, and they ran his underwear up the pole.

Now Scott and Devon pushed the La-Z-Boy off the canoe and began to drag it up Underwear Hill. The recliner was heavy; it snagged in the undergrowth. It slammed into rocks. It got jammed between trees. They accidentally dragged it over a wasp's nest.

They were stung half a dozen times before they could push it away. They went straight through a red anthill. By the time they got to the top of Underwear Hill, they were sweaty, itchy, bitten, and boiling. But proud. They had pulled off the greatest prank in the history of Snow's Pond.

They started laughing when Aunt Sheri pulled up the next day. She was going to be so mad. But she didn't notice the chair. Even when they started making up reasons for her to look across the lake at Underwear Hill, she didn't notice anything amiss. The hill was kind of far away, they realized, and the chair that had looked so huge on the canoe, and felt so huge when being lugged through a wasp's nest, looked really small in the forest. Finally, they gave her a pair of binoculars and told her to look across the lake at . . . a bald eagle or something.

She stared through the binoculars, scanning the woods. She stopped, paused, swung back. Her mouth dropped open. She dropped the binoculars and looked at her nephews, who burst into hysterical laughter.

"Boys," she said, "do you mean to tell me you put that hideous chair in your truck? You drove it up here. You rowed it across the lake. And you hauled it up to the top of that hill."

By now, Devon and Scott were laughing so hard, they could barely stand up.

Aunt Sheri just shook her head, laughing. "What a waste of time."

But was it? After Devon died, and I begged Scott to tell me stories about him, the La-Z-Boy story was the first thing that came to his mind. Is anything that makes a memory, that makes us laugh when we're so deep in mourning, a waste of time?

It might seem like Devon and I never had a fight. That we had a "perfect" relationship, whatever that means. I've wanted us to seem that way. I've wanted to preserve our time together in amber, to present it as perfection. But it isn't quite true. We never bickered over the little things, but we had a calamity, an iceberg-meet-*Titanic* moment, and it almost sank us.

We are real people, after all.

This was the January after my summer internship. I was in law school in Nova Scotia, but there was a last dying flare-up of Covid, and the university decided to go online for six weeks. So I moved to St. John's for a month, to the town house I had recently bought and rented to my brother. Devon was living at his mom's house, but moved some things over to stay with me.

This was the start of our real lives together, when we moved past the magic of our first summer and started to know each other more deeply. Devon saw that I was an anxious person, a perfectionist too hard on herself. I think that's why he complimented me so often, why he was my biggest hype-man: He saw the good in me, and he wanted me to see it in myself.

I saw a sadness in Devon, the struggle behind his cheerful demeanor. He was always on with others, but that winter, with me, I saw how his relentless positivity took something out of him. He was almost always Devon, even in private—the upbeat golden retriever so many people knew and loved. But sometimes he was tired. He was quiet. Contemplative, maybe. Struggling with private thoughts. Never angry or mean, that wasn't Devon, but a little bit withdrawn.

Maybe that's why, when I stumbled on a page of his messages while borrowing his laptop for a school assignment, I stopped for a second and read them. I never suspected I'd find anything amiss, but there were conversations with women whose names I didn't recognize.

I was confused. Were they his friends? Why had he never mentioned them?

I knew in my heart—I suspected, but really, I knew—that there was no innocent answer. And I was stunned. I felt closer to Devon than I ever had with anyone. I trusted him. I *loved him*. Why would he betray my trust?

When he came home, I told him what I'd read.

He didn't argue. He didn't try to explain. He apologized.

So it was real. What I read, what I suspected, it was real.

I told him to get out. He left. The weight, the shock, in those moments after he was gone, when I realized how badly I was hurt. When I sat alone with that deep, deep wound.

The doorbell rang. I didn't want to answer it, but I did. It was Kathleen. She looked me over. She saw my pain. I fell into her hug. Devon's cousins might have been his brothers, but Kathleen was his best friend. The other part of his soul. He had called her as he was leaving and told her what he had done.

"Take care of Laura," Devon told her. "Please make sure she is okay."

Devon went home and told his mother what he had done. He called my father and confessed to him what he had done. Devon knew how much my father meant to me. He didn't want me to have to explain. He wanted my father's first words to be, "I know. I heard. How can I support you?"

A few days later, Devon asked to come back and talk to me. I wasn't sure I wanted to talk to him, but I needed to understand. The chats I'd seen weren't sexual. They were casually flirty. So why do it? Why keep this secret from me?

Devon sat on my sofa, where days before I had read a book while he watched basketball. He hung his head. For a long time, he didn't look up from the floor, which wasn't like Devon. He was the king of eye contact.

He told me that sometimes, a lot of the time, he felt bad about himself.

That he struggled with his eating habits, his exercise.

That sometimes, when I wasn't around, he binged.

That when he was really low and too ashamed to tell me, he would seek validation online.

He wasn't good enough for me, Devon said. He hid his doubts, his hurts, because if I knew how much he struggled, I wouldn't love him. Nobody would.

He stopped right there. He waited. I knew he was ashamed. I didn't respond. I let his words crash over me, absorbing what I could. I knew Devon had body image issues. The signs were obvious.

I knew he had down periods. I knew they were sometimes severe. Once, when he was in university, his mother had flown out to stay with him for a week, because she was afraid.

He said she overreacted, and I was sure he was right. But you never know. You never really know anyone, do you?

I thought I knew Devon. I thought I knew him better than anyone. But I didn't really know him until that night when I realized Devon loved everybody. *Everybody.* Except himself.

I told him I needed to be alone. I knew what he was telling me was true, and I thought of all the times he'd warned me that it was always his fault, he had sabotaged every relationship he'd ever been in. Was he doing that now? Was he blowing up what we had because it was real, and he cared about it deeply, and he was afraid of being hurt by it?

Or did I just want to think that because I was in love with him?

In the end, the decision took weeks, but it came easy, because a throughline of all my self-reflection was one overwhelming wish, one thought that wouldn't go away: I want to help Devon through this. I want to show him he can be loved. That he deserves to be loved. I want him to understand that neither of us is perfect, but that's what makes us perfect for each other.

I wanted to hug him and tell him, forever, for every day, *I love you, Devon, so many people love you, just the way you are.*

THERE ARE SO many, many things I miss about Devon. He was handsome. He was funny. He was a great dog dad. He was my best friend. But the thing I am most in awe of, and will forever be in awe of, is his kindness.

He came by it honestly. I remember how his grandmother

Lulu, stuck in the hospital, went on and on about the food. How delicious it was. How much she appreciated it.

When the nurse came in, Lulu said, "You look so lovely in that outfit."

The nurse looked at her funny. "These are my scrubs," she said. Then she smiled. "But you should see me when I get dressed up to go out."

Yes, Lulu was recovering from an infection. She was a little spacey. But she had been a nurse for her whole working life. She knew what wearing that uniform was like.

And Lulu was Devon's father's mother. The Snow's Pond crew was equally nice. When I first met Devon, and he took me to family gatherings of twenty or thirty strangers, every single person was kind. Every person, every time.

Devon loved basketball. He grew up playing every day. In junior high, his travel team was invited to a prestigious tournament in Las Vegas. He was the consummate teammate: the first to celebrate good plays, the first to console after mistakes. He had a different high-five routine with every player. He had a catalogue of celebrations. He never played a second in Las Vegas. He was the last guy on the bench.

"We called him 'the Glue Stick,'" his cousin Brett, one of the stars of the team, told me. "We couldn't have won without him. He made it fun. Devon made us believe in ourselves."

You aren't born a "Glue Stick," a person who can take disappointment and turn it into genuine enthusiasm for the success of others. You have to make yourself that way. Through empathy and understanding. Through noticing and caring. And almost always, I'd argue, through hurt.

Devon was obsessive about his health. He loved running. It was his passion. He used an app that tracked his times and connected him with runners all over the world. He chatted with them—he encouraged them—every day. It hurt me to learn that he'd started running because he thought he was overweight, and that's why he lost all of his friends. It hurt me to discover that his great passion had started, at least in part, as punishment.

But Devon made it beautiful. I wouldn't trade a single step, a single sunrise he saw while running the Trans-Canada Highway or along the bay, because Devon cherished every step.

The same thing happened with his kindness. Devon had been hurt. At ten, eleven years old he doubted and felt alone. He turned that pain into habit, and that habit into joy. In the same way he monitored his diet, in the same way he monitored his running, Devon became obsessive about being kind.

He listened to everyone. He saw everyone. He took the time to know everyone, to create songs and nicknames, to develop inside jokes. He made everyone feel special, because he knew how much it hurt to be ignored.

My brother, Josh, said it best, and Josh knew the cruel edge of so-called jokes. He grew up gay in Corner Brook, Newfoundland. He was artistic. And well, I used to punch Josh in the face when I was four years old, then walk myself into the time-out room. In middle school, I wouldn't let him speak to me in the halls. Every six months, I write to him and apologize.

He says, *Forget it, Laura. It doesn't matter. We were kids. I'm happy.* But I can't forget it. It can't have been easy for Josh, and I made it worse. So every six months, I apologize again.

"All Devon's joking," Josh said one evening, when we were remembering the man we both adored. "All his nicknames and little songs. They were never meant to hurt. They were never meant to exclude. They were meant to bring you in, to make everyone feel accepted and part of the group."

No, Devon wasn't perfect. Our relationship wasn't perfect. But once I knew how he was broken, I used my love to bind that crack, and he loved me back in the places I was broken, and we were stronger together. Not because we loved the best parts of each other, but because we loved the worst parts, too. Devon never betrayed my trust again. Not once. Not even a little bit. Right up until the moment he died, we had each other's backs.

And after he died, all I could think was, *I am thankful. I am so thankful I loved him through it, and we had our time.*

I HAD HEARD so much about Snow's Pond, I pictured a castle. I was shocked when Devon took me there, and it was a ramshackle cabin. The lake was serene, but the dock was barely long enough for a canoe. Underwear Hill was a bump. The rock wall was exactly as it had been left by "Smash and Dash": wonky and tumbledown, a monument to the foolishness of childhood. The family had wired the cabin for electricity, but they still drew water from the lake, and the only other improvements were the kind of projects homeowners do themselves, with love, over a long series of too-short, too-distracted summers.

When Uncle Jim gave her the property, Devon told me, Aunt

Sue had big ideas. She had an architect draw up plans. Then Devon and her sons sat her down and explained that Snow's Pond was perfect, and she wasn't allowed to touch a thing. The one weekend I spent with Devon at Snow's Pond, we slept in the same bunk beds he'd slept in as a kid, in the same small bedroom. We sat on the same half-broken, swaybacked 1990s couch. When the boys said they wanted nothing to change, they meant nothing. They wanted to preserve Snow's Pond forever, exactly as it had been in the best moments of their lives.

How much of reality is perception? How much of memory is shaped by emotional truth? Does it matter that the boards are crooked, the mattress springs shot?

Of course not. Don't fall for the Instagram post, it isn't real. The wear, the tear, the *living in and living through* is what makes it magic.

SARAH WANTED TO scream on a mountain. That's exactly what she said: "I want to scream on a mountain." So we consulted her book of maps, and the next morning we were on the car ferry across the Carlington Lough to Northern Ireland. On the far shore, there was a ruined castle, a big square block of crumbling stone. It's Ireland. What else would there be? "Some historical information available," read the first review online, "as well as a public toilet."

We drove an hour to the Mourne Area of Outstanding Natural Beauty. It's a wee mountainous region, set amid the rolling hills of eastern Ireland. The terrain reminded me of the mountains outside Corner Brook: stony and round, hard-looking, gray but covered with grass and tough green gorse. Since there are no trees, you can see forever, and it's hard stony hills all the way around.

The weather was reminiscent of Newfoundland, too: a precipitation not quite rain, more wet air. By the time we reached the parking lot, a fog had settled in. It was early September, but it was so cold I bundled under my toque and the Taylor Swift Sweater I had bought during my Personal Boutique Shopping Experience. The toque was hot pink, not my usual color. I bought it after Devon died, hoping the cheerful vibrancy would rub off on my mood. The Taylor Swift Sweater was an Anine Bing.

When we started dating, I started stealing Devon's hoodies, because they were baggy and comfortable. Then he started stealing my oversized hoodies, because he liked how fitted they were on him. When we went to Hawaii, I bought him a hoodie and promised not to steal it. After that, every time we traveled, I bought Devon a hoodie. Devon's favorite was the Muhammad Ali hoodie I bought him on our trip to Florida with Reb and Kyle. My Anine Bing was like Muhammad Ali, a wearable souvenir.

I zipped it beneath a heavy jacket and started up the valley. The trail rose steadily, leaving a stream behind as it wound around the mountain. It wasn't a hard hike, but after forty minutes in the cold and the wet, we'd had enough. The day was lousy. There were only a few people around. I'd like to say we were at the peak, but we were more like three-quarters of the way.

"This is the place," Sarah said, and she and Lucy started

screaming. A hiker on another hill almost fell down, he was so startled. Lucy and Sarah kept screaming. For Devon.

I couldn't do it. Devon used to say I never had to raise my voice to get what I wanted, not with him, and not with anyone. On the mountain, I realized he was right. I'm not a yeller.

I also don't curse. It's not like I come from a long line of G-rated Baymen, there's no such thing. My family curses plenty. But I don't like it.

Don't yell. Don't curse. Be nice.

"We passed a dam back there," Sarah said. It was more a flood lock, but sure. "Just yell about that."

I didn't want to, but I tried.

"Dam," I said.

"Dam!"

"DAM!"

"DAMN IT!"

God damn it, world, why did you do this? Why? What did I do? Damn you.

Sarah took out her phone for a video. It's the three of us, crowded together into the frame. We're a little awkward. A little stiff, because of the camera. But we're screaming loud, and I'm dropping a shocking number of F-bombs.

I don't know if it did me any good. I don't know if any of this is doing me any good. There were important words unspoken when I left Ireland, a regret that ate away at me for months and months until I came home from my honeymoon and finally confronted a guilt I didn't have the courage to face when we were alone in Carlingford.

I took Sarah's son away. I took him across the island of Newfoundland to be with me. And he died there, in my arms, four hundred miles from her home.

"I'm sorry, Sarah," I blurted one night, as the grief came crashing out of me. "I'm so sorry I didn't save him."

She pulled me close. "Oh, Laura," she said. "You did."

Arizona

What is a wedding without the engagement, even if the wedding never takes place? What is an engagement to a hopeless romantic like Devon O'Grady, if not the chance of a lifetime? What can these so-called special moments, these big gestures, tell us about all the other ordinary moments, like reading the misadventures of a Sally Rooney heroine in love while your fiancé watches a basketball game played twenty hours ago, or when you can't read anymore, as much as you try, because you're too distracted thinking about your fiancé watching television, and crying because you'll never get to watch him watching basketball again?

It started with the ring. Devon made sure it was special. He gathered the gold from old family jewelry. He took pearls from a pair of Sarah's earrings, because I once casually mentioned that I liked pearls on rings. Devon loved pearls. He wore his mother's old pearl necklace around his neck until he lost it one day while we were on a hike with the dogs. The four closest women in his life—Sarah, Kathleen, Lucy, and Jamie, Lucy's daughter—each contributed a diamond from necklaces given to them by Sarah years ago. The ring was designed and forged, with Devon's input, in Toronto by a cousin's friend.

It ended, of course, with the drop to one knee. Devon made sure that was special, too. It was March, about eight months after

Janine's wedding, and we were traveling to Arizona with my family for a winter getaway. Devon was going to propose to me there, but he didn't have a specific spot in mind. As I said, he wasn't a planner. It was very like Devon to assume he'd find the perfect moment on a desert hike, with a gorgeous view of a sunset or, if he could rouse me out of bed, sunrise. For Devon, who had a way of making every moment special, winging it was an acceptable plan.

Then a winter storm blew in, and it looked like our flight might be canceled. Typical March weather for St. John's. Devon tried to move our tickets up a day to avoid the storm, but the timetable was tight, and the airline was inundated with calls. We thought we were doomed. Which is fine, sometimes plans don't come together. But a few minutes after midnight, Devon was able to move our tickets to that morning. We threw our bags together and rushed to the airport. We were on different flights. Devon was leaving an hour before me (at 4:30 A.M.). It wasn't until we got to the airport that we realized, in the rush, Devon had forgotten to check me in online. I had been bumped to standby.

Devon tried to swap tickets with me, but the airline wouldn't let him. He tried to skip his flight and stay with me, but I wouldn't let him. He flew off to Toronto for our connecting flight, convinced I wasn't going to make it onto a plane before the storm.

I made it, the last one off the standby list. It was such a close call, I forgot to text Devon and tell him I was on the flight. I arrived in Toronto about nine in the morning. I hadn't slept. I was exhausted. I was starving. Devon was waiting at the gate, hoping I was on that plane. As soon as I saw him, I knew everything was going to be okay.

He took me to Denny's for breakfast. Then we went to the cheapo hotel he had booked near the airport, because we had flown in a day early and our next flight wasn't until tomorrow, and took a nap.

I was in bed, disheveled, with the sheet piled around me, when I saw Devon drop to one knee. He held out a box. I knew it was the ring.

He made a speech. I'm sure it was a good one: spontaneous, funny, heartfelt. I didn't hear it, because I was bawling. Devon surprised me, that's for sure. I expected a proposal, but not right then. Not in *Mississauga*. Devon said the delay, the worry, had convinced him there was no time to waste. Time, after all, is the most precious thing we have.

We searched the internet for a fancy restaurant. We figured we should treat ourselves to a nice engagement dinner. But all the restaurants that sounded good were in Toronto, an hour and an expensive Uber ride away. We decided to walk next door to the Keg, a chain steakhouse. I'd FaceTimed Reb after Devon's proposal. She was expecting it. She and Devon had been texting about it for weeks. But she never thought it would happen in Mississauga. This was the man, after all, who took me on a first date to see the sunrise over the ocean. Who spread a picnic at the edge of a cliff so we could watch the sunset over a different side of the ocean at the end of our first summer together. A man like Devon doesn't propose in Mississauga.

When Reb heard we were going to the Keg, she called them and ordered us a bottle of champagne. Unfortunately, the Keg is not the kind of place that takes credit card orders over the phone. They did, however, bring us two free glasses of champagne, so Devon and I toasted our engagement in the mostly empty dining room of the Mississauga outpost of Canada's (probably) most popular steakhouse chain. It wasn't an invigorating hike and a sunrise over the desert, but we did get the primo table in front of the artificial fire.

That's the story I told, anyway, and I would have gone on telling it that way, especially in this book. I have struggled, mightily, with writing about Devon. Especially the tougher chapters like Devon breaching my trust. I worked on that chapter for months, and I'll never be totally comfortable with it. But the things that matter, everyone tells me, are the things that hurt the most. And that one hurts. But I struggle with the lesser things, too, the positive things. It's not shame or wanting to protect him; it's that Devon isn't here to tell me it's okay.

Who am I to tell Devon's story without him? What gives me the right to tell anyone's story, other than my own? How can I be sure I'm telling it right? How do I know I'm not doing harm—to you, to me, to the man I love?

I don't care what you think about me after reading this book. I really don't. But I can't hurt Devon. I just can't. I have to make you understand the man he was, no matter what you think of me.

Devon, though. My Dev—he was irrepressible. He told the whole story of our engagement, and he told it often, and that story is that we had some pretty fantastic sex in that hotel room, and we were naked, sweaty, and disheveled when he proposed.

Devon told that R-rated version to everybody: my mom, his mom, my sister, his sister. When people at work asked . . . we looked at each other and laughed, and told them Devon proposed during a layover in Mississauga. I'm not sure if my father was told the most famous version, although clearly he knows it now.

And you know what? I don't mind. Not every moment has to be a sunrise to be special. It simply has to be sincere.

Bath

MY MOTHER'S FAMILY goes way back in Corner Brook, paper mill and railroad workers, a few loggers, too. Corner Brook is a paper mill town. The property she inherited from Pop, her father, had been in the family for generations. It was in Steady Brook, a village of a few hundred people a few miles outside Corner Brook. It was three homesteads wide and backed up to the Humber River. Pop's sister lived on the left-most plot. Mom lived in the middle. On the third lot, she built a house to sell. It was bought by a family from England, as a vacation home.

I was ten the summer of their first visit, and I thought their daughter, Romy, was the coolest kid I had ever met. She had a British accent. She had loads of British candy, like Percy Pigs. I was shy, but Romy and I had an instant connection. Whenever Romy's family was in town, I spent all my time at Mom's house, so I could spend all my time at Romy's house, which was full of CDs and books. At school, I wasted hours thinking about hanging out with Romy, and she must have been thinking the same, because as soon as my bus pulled up she would come running out the door, and we'd race to the fort we had built down by the river to chat, pop Percy Pigs, and read Romy's vast collection of British teen magazines.

Romy's parents took me on their family trips to Gros Morne, the only national park on the west coast of the island. We spent a few days looking for moose, eating poutine, hiking the giant chunk of the earth's mantle that thrusts up out in the wilderness, like a barren, magnesium-red mountain. Moose and poutine: Romy's favorite Canadian things.

Our families got along well. We went hiking, fishing, camping, skiing. We spent many, many evenings playing Pass the Pigs, a game where you roll two pigs like dice and score based on how the pigs land—snout, side, butt, head, etc. We loved Pass the Pigs so much that last year, for Christmas, Romy gave each person in my family their own game. Percy Pigs, Pass the Pigs, poutine: Life with Romy was good. I thought we'd be eating Percy Pigs together forever.

Then, when we were in high school, Romy's father died unexpectedly. The family never came back to Newfoundland. Eventually, they sold the house. Over the next ten years, I saw Romy only once. But we stayed in touch over Messenger, and then FaceTime. We got engaged a few months apart. We planned our weddings for the same summer. We spent the spring messaging back and forth, discussing important things like flowers and bridesmaids' gifts and the rest of our lives.

When Devon died, Romy messaged me: Laura, my heart is broken for you. There are no words. Nothing is enough. I am desperately sorry and I love you xx

I sent her a picture from the top of Marble Mountain: me, with a backpack on, looking out at the view. Inside the backpack were Devon's ashes.

> I carried him to the top
> It reminds me of you up there as well as we went there together

You are beautiful, Laura, she wrote back. How incredibly brave of you.

Romy came to Devon's Celebration of Life. She never met Devon in person, but she knew him. Everyone who knew me knew Devon, and knew how much he meant to me.

Afterward, she sent me a care package: a sleep mask, bath bombs, scents for sleeping, toys and treats for the dogs . . . and Percy Pigs. Romy was like that. If I complimented anything, like her phone case, she sent me one, with a handwritten note. If I mentioned anything I needed, even in passing, she sent it to me. Romy understood the comfort of Percy Pigs.

If you're wondering why my honeymoon was two months after my wedding date, it was because of Romy. Devon and I hadn't planned much of our honeymoon, but we knew we wanted our first stop to be Romy's wedding. It was going to be perfect. I was going to get married, then fly to England and watch Romy get married, a special friend I hadn't seen in person in six years. Even a week before I left for London, I insisted I was going to Romy's wedding.

Then I came to my senses. I couldn't watch my friend walk down the aisle to happiness, I realized, without crashing. It was a horrible realization: I couldn't be happy for Romy, because I'd be too heartbroken for myself. It's something I've had to accept: Grief makes you selfish, and that's okay.

So while I was eating McDonald's French fries with drunk American girls, Romy was celebrating the happiest day of her life. While I was buying a $26 cocktail at *Phantom of the Opera* and struggling through a week on the French Riviera, Romy was enjoying her honeymoon in Greece.

We were out of sync. I had fallen out of time.

Our schedules finally worked out after Ireland. Romy was back from her honeymoon, and I had a few days before my next stop: Italy. The joy in my heart when I saw her: It was like being back under the covers with a flashlight, checking out the (terrible) 2000s fashions in *Sugar* magazine. We had a great conversation on the way to her house in a planned community outside Bath, which she and her husband, Sam, had bought that spring.

Sam was a good man, easygoing and kind. He had the shaggy brown hair of vintage Harry Styles, and a terrific British accent. He carried my suitcase. He made us coffee. He and Romy had been together since high school, and they were comfortable and affectionate, but not too affectionate. I could tell Romy didn't want me to think about her relationship, about how nicely her life was falling into place. She had thought through everything, even my emotional needs. Even the shameful jealousy and sadness I'd feel when I saw how happy she was with Sam.

And yet, when I looked around their house, their love was there: Centerpieces from their reception shoved into a corner, vases of dying flowers not yet thrown away. Wedding presents piled in the hallway, still wrapped. They hadn't even taken the bow off their new life together.

"Are you okay?" Romy said.

"Just tired," I said. It was true. I was exhausted. Grief will pound you like a prize fighter. Romy took me to my bedroom upstairs. The bed was covered in Percy Pigs.

I started to cry. I gave Romy a hug.

"I love you," I said.

WHEN I WAS two years old, I lost the ability to walk. Every time I tried, I cried. My parents took me to a series of doctors, who diagnosed rheumatoid arthritis. My ankle joints were inflamed, making it painful for me to toddle around doing two-year-old things.

There's medicine to control the symptoms of rheumatoid arthritis, but no cure. Most of my life, I've been uncomfortable, but I managed. I played sports. Not well, but I played. Periodically, though, the pain was debilitating. Sometimes the disease had progressed, but at other times, the symptoms were triggered by stress. When I was nine, my mother was diagnosed with cancer, and my arthritis became so bad it hurt to walk. The doctors put me on stronger medication, but my symptoms didn't go away until my mother's cancer went into remission and I knew she was going to be okay.

By high school, my discomfort was close to constant, and my wrists were weak. I ignored it. When my doctors switched me to biologics, which required weekly injections, I wasn't diligent about giving myself the shots. I was too busy hanging out with Reb and throwing parties (sorry again, Dad). My mother, Sammy Walsh, had always been the healer in her family. No one was surprised when she became a nurse. She made it her mission to take care of me. She administered my injections. She prepared hot compresses for my joints. She talked to my doctors. She cooked me healthy meals. And I got better. I don't think many people, outside of Reb and Janine, knew the severity of my condition.

I wasn't a top student in high school. I didn't raise my hand in class or try my hardest because I wanted to fit in. I didn't start working hard until my junior year, and that was because Josh graduated with honors, and if my older brother did it, that meant I had to do it, too. We were very competitive with each other. I keep it hidden, but I'm a very competitive person. And stubborn, like my dad.

And I'm not sure Josh knows this, but I've always looked up to him. When I punched him in the face at four years old, it was because he wouldn't play with me, and I was desperate to play with my big brother. I couldn't let him beat me, not at school, not at anything.

I graduated with honors. I got a scholarship to university. It felt good. It felt like the real Laura Murphy, so I kept working hard. Rigorous studying, no partying. (Okay, limited partying.) I interned with a professor. Later, I interned with a senator. I spent most of a year working on a research study at a facility for those declared not guilty by reason of mental disorder. My body began breaking down, but it wasn't the work. It was that, by college, I had been on biologics for years, and their efficacy weakens over time. My wrists were increasingly sore, my jaw increasingly tight. When I have a rheumatic episode, I get a pain in the hinge of my jaw. When it gets bad, I struggle to chew and swallow. I kept going, pushing through the pain as I always had, until the morning I was forced to call my mother.

"Mom," I said. "I can't get out of bed."

She rushed to Halifax from Corner Brook, a journey that included a seven-hour ferry ride. By the time she arrived, I was out of bed, but it hurt so much to walk I had only made it to one of my four classes. Mom lifted me under the arms and coaxed me into a hot bath. She bought medicinal salts. She put hot towels around my neck, tucked up against my aching jaw. My arthritis had flared in forty-eight joints: my wrists, elbows, jaw, hips, ankles, spine, neck. I hurt *everywhere*.

I remember lying in the bath, which eased the worst of my pain, and thinking: It's okay. If I can't do anything else, I can still use my brain.

My mother practically carried me to doctors' appointments. She walked me to my bath each night. The doctors kept changing my medicine, but my symptoms didn't improve. I was forced to drop a class. That sent me into an emotional spiral.

No law school will take me now, I thought. I won't even be able to use my brain.

A therapist put me on antidepressants. I am still on them today.

A natural healer recommended I give up dairy, sugar, and gluten. The dairy and sugar didn't stick, but without gluten I felt better.

My mother stayed with me in Halifax off and on for months, cooking, cleaning, and administering my shots. When I was younger, I resented her focus on healthy eating. I don't want almonds for a snack! I want a cheeseburger! Dad grills cheeseburgers all the time. But when I needed her—when I really needed a mother to take care of me—she was there. She did all the hard little things.

But I was still in pain.

Finally, a doctor recommended rituximab. It's a lymphoma medicine, but it's known to treat autoimmune diseases. There's a seven-level scale for the treatment of rheumatoid arthritis. By switching to rituximab, I was moving up to level seven, the strongest possible treatment. I had to go to a cancer center. I had to sign a waiver about potentially fatal brain infections. Twenty-one years old, and I was already gambling my brain, with no guarantee the treatment would be effective.

It worked.

Thank you, modern medicine. It worked.

Within a couple of months, the worst of my symptoms had cleared. I got my body back. I got my life as a college student back. Then I was accepted into law school, and I got my brain back, too. After graduation, I went backpacking with a friend to Southeast Asia and Australia. I was pain-free. I was living again.

The protocol is simple. I go to a treatment center for two infusions, administered two weeks apart, every six months. Each infusion takes six hours, like chemo. If I go in on time, I don't have symptoms, but sometimes outside issues cause delays, and the arthritis symptoms come back. The infusion weakens my immune system, so I almost always get sick. But after that, my physical ailments clear for another six months.

There are side effects, although I never know what they will be. I've had asthma. I've had allergic reactions. My face swells up like a balloon when I have to take prednisone to relieve the pain.

Once, the skin around my eyes peeled off. It disintegrated in white shreds, with raw skin underneath.

Devon said, "You're beautiful."

He didn't say, It's fine. He didn't say, It's temporary. He said, "You're beautiful," and I could hear it in his voice: You're beautiful right now, Laura, and if your skin stays like that for the rest of your life, you'll be beautiful on all those days, too.

And I'll always love you exactly as you are.

I thought about those two simple words that night as I lay in a bed of Percy Pigs, arthritis clawing at the hinge of my jaw, since I was months overdue for my next set of shots.

You're beautiful.

I thought of the way Devon looked at me whenever he said it. Like he loved me, with a love barely contained. I mean, I knew Devon loved me, but it still stopped my heart whenever he stopped and turned to me, as if he couldn't go another second without letting me know: "Laura Murphy, I love you. You're beautiful."

Only Devon could make me believe it.

SAM COOKED US breakfast, the full English. Eggs. Baked beans. No blood sausage but bacon, mushrooms, tomatoes, and toast. Romy and I sat at their coffee table, because Sam and Romy didn't have a kitchen table yet, and drank coffee while he worked. Sam had it brewed for us by the time I got up. There wasn't much furniture in the house, but the kitchen was fully stocked.

Devon and I had often talked about moving to Bath, usually right after one of my FaceTimes with Romy, which Devon was always crashing. It wasn't realistic. It was more a distant possibility. Sarah was a British citizen, so Devon was a citizen, and he liked to imagine an English village, a little house with a garden plot, and a snug around the corner. Barrister, we'd call each other. Barrister O'Grady, as if the British legal system still operated like it was 1953. As Devon always said: Why not?

It was sort of his life's philosophy: Why not dream big? Why not believe? *Why not?*

Romy wanted to give me a tour of Bath in the hopes I'd fall in love with it and be her neighbor again. Bath is an old city, famous for the Circus, a circle of stately white town houses, ideally proportioned and almost exactly alike, with a park in the center. The inner ring was designed to be the same size as the outer circle of monoliths at Stonehenge. We walked it three times. There's also an opera house in Bath, an ancient bridge, the Royal Crescent. Most of the historic stuff is named after kings and queens, or at least high society, since Bath has always been a . . . bath town. Rich people and royalty have been coming to enjoy the local springs and spas since Roman times. Even in 2024, people dressed like Elizabeth Bennet and Mr. Darcy, as if they'd stepped directly off a country estate in 1813.

It turned out a Jane Austen festival was being held in town, and these were superfans. Still, if you were dreaming of moving to England, Bath was the kind of place you pictured. An old-money town—as in money that paid for buildings two hundred fifty years ago. That's when the Circus was completed: 1768.

I tried to picture myself living in a town like this. What would life be like on this block? Walking this route every day? In this coffee shop?

I'm a small-town Newfie. I've lived in Halifax, Nova Scotia, the largest city in Atlantic Canada, and loved it. I've stayed with my brother in Toronto. I've traveled to a dozen places, and had a great time almost everywhere, but I never seriously considered moving anywhere. There's just something about my big rock in the North Atlantic, where my roots are deep. It has always felt like home. Until Devon came along, with his "we can do anything" attitude, I figured I'd settle in Newfoundland and live there forever.

But I loved England. I loved walking through new places, seeing new things. I loved the idea of getting away from the suffocating sadness of Corner Brook, where everyone hovered over me, crushing me with their kindness and expectations. I craved a new start, a new country, with one good friend nearby.

But where? London, with its vibes? Or Bath, with Romy and Sam and Jane Austen's superfans?

DEVON LIKED TO talk about poop and farts. That's what his niece Bailey said when I sat down to talk with her about her uncle. The first time I met Bailey was when she peppered me with questions at her dog-themed seventh birthday party. She thought Devon was cool, so she assumed I was cool, and none of the dorky stuff I'd done in the three years since could convince her she was wrong.

We were close, Bailey and me. We texted on her mom's phone. We went shopping for clothes or on ice cream dates. We went to the movies. Whenever there was a family event or a weekend at North River, Bailey sought me out and sat beside me, talking my ear off.

When her parents asked what she wanted for her tenth birthday, Bailey said she wanted to spend the day with me. A ten-year-old kid wanting to see her almost-aunt more than, say, getting tickets to Taylor Swift!

This was eight weeks after Devon died. It was a dark time. Bailey lived in St. John's. That was seven hours away, and that was Devon's town. I was Laura the Wet Blanket Thrown in a Pile in the Corner. (That's worse than a regular wet blanket.) I was barely sliding out of bed, except to jog myself to exhaustion with my father. Even the supermarket seemed impossibly far. I had to tell her mother I couldn't make it.

But I didn't feel right about it. So I texted Kathleen and asked if she could be there for me. I drove the seven hours to Kathleen and Sarah's row house. Kathleen drove me to Bailey's house. A block away, we stopped, and I put a gift bag over my head.

I heard the front door open as our car pulled up, then footsteps running down the walk as Kathleen got out of the driver's seat and slammed the door behind her. Kathleen had told Bailey she was coming over with a gift. Bailey had clearly been waiting.

"Happy birthday," Kathleen said.

"What is it?"

"It's in the car."

"What is it?"

Then I heard Bailey scream: "It's Laura!"

"No, it's not," Kathleen said.

"Yes, it is; yes, it is." I could hear Bailey jumping, screaming at the top of her lungs. "It's Laura! It's Laura!"

I started bawling under my bag. Not from sadness, from appreciation. As soon as Bailey lifted off the bag, "unwrapping" her present, I leaned over and hugged her, partly so she wouldn't see my tears, partly to thank her for this fierce devotion that I have no idea what I did to earn. I hope one day, when she's older, Bailey will understand how much this meant to me.

I hope her brother, Kai, and all Devon's other nieces and nephews, know how much they mean to me, too. I love spending time with Kai, listening to his sidewinding stories about kids from his school and karate. Such a kid's-eye view of the world.

But Bailey, she had a wall of Devon photographs in her bedroom. DEVON TRIBUTE WALL, it said on a piece of paper taped at the top. There was a letter she wrote to Devon after he died. There was a drawing of one of Devon's famous basketball shoes, with their bright green laces. Devon was obsessive about his shoes.

Bailey wrote me letters, too.

Bailey made motivational videos and posted them every Monday to a private text chat. They were meant to cheer me up, but soon half the family was watching them.

Bailey begged to be in our wedding, before we had even thought about the details of our wedding, and of course I said yes. After that, it was an open invitation affair. Anyone who wanted to be in our wedding, Devon and I said yes.

"Devon made me a sandwich with everything on it," Bailey said in her speech at Devon's Celebration of Life, and again as I sat in her parents' living room asking for stories about him.

I remember that day. Devon was out for a run, and by the time he got back, I was laid out on the couch with a headache. I asked him to get my computer from our nightstand. When he got to the bedroom, Bailey jumped out and surprised him.

She was so happy. She had planned the headache, the computer, the whole thing. She and Devon went on and on about it, discussing how surprised he'd been.

Afterward, we realized she hadn't eaten lunch. Devon and I had a careful diet: vegetables, gluten-free bread, no processed meat or snacks. There was nothing in our house for a kid.

So Devon started pulling things out of the refrigerator: green peppers, carrots, cucumbers, cheese, hummus, salad dressing, even butter and ketchup. Even the oranges. He got out two pieces of bread. He started spreading sauces and cutting up vegetables.

"What's that?" Bailey asked.

"It's a sandwich with everything on it."

"You can't do that," she said with a laugh.

"Sure, you can."

He held up the sandwich. Bailey looked at it skeptically. It was dripping with sauces and big green vegetable chunks. "I'm not going to eat that," she said.

"Sure, you are," Devon said, and took a humongous bite. Bailey's eyes popped out of her head. "It's delicious."

"No, it's not."

Devon took another huge bite. "You gonna try it?"

"Oh, ugh, it's gross, it's so gross," she said between bites, but barely, because she was so busy laughing.

That's Devon, he had a way with kids. He knew how to talk to them. It wasn't just gross foods or poop jokes; kids are smarter than that. They understand when you're distracted, when you're hurrying, when you're telling them what they want to hear. They loved "Uncle Deevs" because he was present. He paid attention. He loved talking with them about farts, sure, but also tons of other stuff, as much as they loved talking to him.

Devon wanted kids. He talked about it all the time. He was so fired up to be a dad.

What's the hurry? I said. We're young. We're in love with our lives.

We have time.

I WAS TRYING to check my socials only in the evening. TikTok was bombarding me with notifications, but I wanted to stay in the moment, not on my phone. By the time I looked at my account each night, there were hundreds of new comments. Romy read through them with me and was appalled. So many creepy men. So many trolls. So many links to predatory news articles.

Eh, I thought, that's social media. Don't let it get you down.

Life is what you look for, after all, what you choose to pick out from all the detritus flowing by you, and I was searching for the sufferers: the young widows, the grieving parents, those struggling through a life-altering event. My people. The ones who made me feel less alone. They made me feel like all this traveling, all these posts, had meaning.

Then I noticed the article about my honeymoon had been

published in *The Washington Post.* That stopped me, because this wasn't the internet. It was real. I clicked on the article and, after a deep breath, started reading. Halfway through, I was crying. By the end, I was in full meltdown, the seventh wave of the seventh waves: a crusher.

It was beautifully written.

There was a picture of Devon, smiling that gorgeous Devon smile.

The reporter understood. She cared. She had gotten (almost) everything right.

And that's what killed me. It's real, I thought. Oh my god, it's real. I am this tragic girl, the one the newspaper has verified and reflected back at me.

I can't believe this is my life.

DEVON AND I interviewed with Poole Althouse, the law firm in Corner Brook where my father had been the senior partner before becoming a judge. They had lost several junior associates, and they were desperate to hire young lawyers. It's hard to recruit good lawyers to a small town like Corner Brook, Newfoundland. Getting two from a top St. John's firm was a rare opportunity. They made it clear they wanted us.

Devon said, Let's do it. Why not? He loved being near his family in St. John's, loved the city, loved hiking the coastal trails on a warm summer weekend, but he was searching for something more in his life. The Growlers had folded after one season. I guess Newfoundland isn't big enough to support a professional basketball team. He was back at Curtis Dawe, but he didn't love it. I'm not sure Devon ever loved being a lawyer. Poole Althouse was a fresh start, but more than that, it was a new life.

"It's peaceful here," Devon argued as we looked out on the Humber River from my father's porch. "We can afford a house with a yard. We can plant a garden. Explore the west coast. Raise honeybees."

Why not?

I wasn't convinced. I loved the idea of going home and being near family, but I loved Curtis Dawe, too. I loved living in St. John's. Well, not the rain. In the winter, the St. John's weather was abominable, while Corner Brook was glorious: white snow on Marble Mountain, skiing, snowshoeing. Moving home, I knew, meant moving into the next phase of our lives: getting married, starting a family. That's the fresh start Devon wanted, not just for himself, but for me. He thought being near my family would make me happy. I thought it would make me happy, too. I just wasn't sure I was ready.

By the last cold rains of April, I'd come around.

Why not, right, Devon?

We moved to Corner Brook in October, when the trees were gold and amber on the mountains. We bought a house with three bedrooms. The Poole Althouse offices were two minutes away. Our offices were across the hall from each other. Mine had a view of a park. Devon's looked out on the dumpster behind the Kentucky Fried Chicken. He had insisted he choose first.

In law firms in small cities, most of the cases come in unsolicited. At Curtis Dawe, the junior lawyers had to filter the cold calls. At Poole Althouse, a group of assistants took the calls. Within days—no, hours—Devon was on a first-name basis with them. Within weeks, they were best friends. Marsha, who Devon called Marshmallow, loved toffee. Devon bought her twelve boxes for Christmas and individually wrapped each one. April's daughter played basketball. Devon offered to help her train. Debbie, Hilda—he loved them, too. He genuinely loved them all, and they knew it. I'm pretty sure they slid him the best calls, the corporate and real estate cases.

I got stuck with divorces. I spent hours listening to people who had once cared about each other argue over a coffee table. Even before I lost Devon, I would sit there thinking, Why? Why hurt each other? Why waste your time? You're paying me three times as much as that table is worth.

Honestly, it probably would have been better if we'd been assigned cases the other way around. I was good at law. Devon was good with people. He would have disarmed their anger in a minute.

That winter, after we'd settled into our new house, and realized our insulation was inadequate and our propane tank outdated, I stopped my birth control. Devon's cousin Brett and his wife were expecting twins. My best friend Janine gave birth in February, and watching Devon hold Presley . . . it was so natural. It was so right.

And I wanted children, almost as much as Devon. But I wanted to wait until we were married. I didn't mind having children outside of marriage. What did that matter? I just didn't want to be pregnant at the wedding. I wanted to fit into my dress. I wanted to drink with my friends and family.

Of all the stupid, terrible . . .

By April, I was ready. Even if I got pregnant right away, which I didn't think I would, I wouldn't be showing at the wedding in June. We started putting in the work. I started thinking about a little girl, a little boy.

"I wish you two had had children," Sarah muttered shortly after Devon died. It wasn't an accusation, and she didn't mean to hurt me. Sarah has never said a single word with the intention of hurting me. It just slipped out, this tragedy eating away at her, this regret deep in her soul.

I know, Sarah. I know. I am so, so sorry. If it were up to Devon, we'd have had a daughter. Maybe a son, too. I should have listened to him. Because I wanted that. I wanted it badly. For you. For me. For Devon.

I just misjudged the time.

ON MY LAST day in Bath, Romy and I drove to Frome, a traditional British village—cobblestone streets, three-hundred-year-old buildings, big shop windows, fish and chips—then on to Longleat House, completed in 1579 and the ancestral home of the Marquess of Bath. It's a typical British estate: a long, straight drive across a very large lawn with a huge rectangular structure full of windows at the end. There's a reflecting pond, a hedge maze. I'm sure the inside is full of plush curtains, tapestries, and chairs. We did not, however, go in. We were there for the safari park.

It was on the grounds of the estate, on the land where, in a romance novel, the heroine would come upon the handsome stable boy—surprise, he's secretly the master of the house!—having fallen off his horse trying to save a rabbit or something, proving he's not the heartless jerk she assumed he was. At Longleat, the rabbits were in the Animal Adventure. It's a petting zoo. We didn't go in. We didn't take the jungle cruise around the artificial lake, where the oldest gorilla in Europe had lived alone on an island until he died the year before.

Instead, we drove Romy's car into the safari lands. I had skipped my last rheumatoid arthritis infusion, back in the spring. It wasn't safe to get pregnant while on my medication. On the day Sarah, Lucy, and I screamed on a mountain, my wrists were so sore I could barely hold my phone. By my first night in Bath, the pain had reached my jaw. Now it was in my ankles and knees, so I was happy to sit for a while and stare out the window. The brochure promised zebras, ostriches, wildebeests, warthogs, and Rothschild's giraffes, which I assume are the fanciest and wealthiest kind.

We saw none of that. It was pouring down rain. It rained almost every day I was in the British Isles, but this was the worst. We could barely see out the windshield. No beast would be out in conditions like that. And yet, we had a blast, scanning the horizon of this bizarre estate for . . .

"Hey, there's a warthog."

Nope, it's a bush.

"Giraffe!"

Nope, a tree, swaying in the storm.

The first animal we saw was a monkey. He came loping alongside Romy's car. He was swinging his arms and pointing to his mouth, like he wanted us to give him food, but that was forbidden. We weren't allowed to roll down our windows, either, but Romy did. She cracked her window a few inches, and that's when the monkey jumped.

He hit Romy's window with a thud and grabbed onto the window frame. We started screaming. He was screaming, baring his teeth. And not just him. Suddenly, there were ten monkeys, maybe twenty. They were hanging off the hood of the car, the front windows, the back windows, screaming—but we were screaming louder. Romy hit the gas in a panic. We were so focused on the monkeys, we barely saw the exit, but as soon as we whizzed through the gate, the monkeys jumped and scattered.

Romy slammed the brakes so hard, I almost hit the windshield. I sat up and looked over at her. She was looking at me. Neither one of us knew what to say. Then we started laughing. Had we really just been menaced by monkeys on a Jane Austen–style English estate?

We were in a holding pen, with a fence on all sides. Staff members were reaching long poles through the fence, poking aggressively at the bottom of Romy's car. Five monkeys dropped off and ran, hopping through a gate back into the preserve. Spiders hiding in crevices was bad enough. But monkeys?

That's when I remembered: Oh yeah, they warned us about the monkeys. They were always trying to escape.

That night, our last together, I introduced Romy to *The Secret Lives of Mormon Wives.*

Newfoundland

OUR FIRST TWO months in Corner Brook were such a whirlwind—new jobs, new house, new life—that we almost missed Christmas. Devon bought gifts for me, for friends, for family, for all the assistants in the office, including those twelve individually wrapped boxes of toffee for Marsha(mallow). He was a great gift giver. He's the only man who has ever given me what I wanted to wear, instead of what he wanted me to wear. We got out a few decorations and other odds and ends. But it was December 23 before we looked up and realized we had missed the centerpiece of the season.

"Let's go," my father said when we told him we didn't have a tree.

Much of Canada, especially rural Canada, is "cut your own" country. We have millions of trees up here, just standing around waiting for the chopping. So it was a familiar memory for me to bundle into Dad's truck in my winter gear and head down the Woods Roads, as we call them—the tracks the logging companies cut into the forests to get the pulp wood for the paper mill—to find a Christmas tree.

For Devon the Townie, it was a brand-new adventure. As he watched the forest roll by, I could sense his excitement, and I began to feel it, too. There was a foot of snow on the ground, fluffy and white. We were so deep in the woods nothing human or modern had touched it, and it was so quiet you could hear the occasional snowpack, heavy with ice, drop from the trees. We stopped every few minutes to check out a young evergreen, but Devon was never satisfied. He wanted to go on, find something better. That was fine with Dad and me. We had our heavy coats and our thermos of coffee, and we had one another.

After about an hour, we came to a clearing, where a dozen small firs were taking advantage of the sunlight. Devon walked the edge, examining each one. "This one," he said finally, and Dad fired up the chainsaw.

Back home, my brother and sister helped us, well . . . repeatedly knock over the tree, which turned out to be precariously balanced. When we finally lifted it straight, it gouged a scar in the ceiling. The tree was an inch too tall. By then, the four of us were laughing so hard, we could barely unpack the strands of lights and boxes of ornaments, many of which were mementos from our childhoods. The decorating was awful. It looked like we were drunk, but none of us had any alcohol.

After Josh and Tamara left, Devon turned off the overheads and clicked off the lamps so the Christmas lights sparkled. We sat in our living room for what felt like hours, as the snow fell lightly and crackled on the windowpane.

"Perfect tree," I said.

Devon nodded. "Perfect tree."

We celebrated New Year's Eve at Dad's house with my family. Kathleen and Sarah came over from St. John's, their first visit since we moved to Corner Brook. Kathleen, who was as good as Devon at putting everyone at ease, masterminded a bunch of games. We played Flip Cup. We tried to blow up balloons with straws. We held a balloon in our teeth and dangled it in a Solo cup. The object was to blow up the balloon so much that it would press against the sides, allowing you to lift the cup without touching anything with your hands. It's incredible, really, how much you can do with balloons and plastic cups. We had so much fun, I can't remember who won.

In St. John's, it was a decades-old tradition for Devon's grandmother and aunt, who lived together, to serve coffee at 11:00 A.M. and tea at 3:00 P.M. every Saturday. Devon and I went every weekend we were in town. There were usually ten or twelve family members there, including Bailey and her brother, Kai, and although Granny's manners were proper, her house was small. We leaned on the arms of chairs, or crammed five deep on the single sofa, or sat cross-legged on the floor, where Granny's blind weiner dog, Nala, would sniff up and down my legs before curling up on my lap and falling asleep.

In Corner Brook, we had lunch with Pop, my mother's father. It started as a simple Saturday invite, but Pop said, "Come by anytime," and Devon took him at his word. I'd be in my office working, and Devon would pop his head in: "Let's go to Pop's for lunch."

Pop was always waiting, with a loaf of homemade bread. Devon adored Pop's homemade bread and berry jams. They would sit at the kitchen table while I made scrambled eggs. Pop read a lot of history. He and I always talked about books. The most ferocious readers in my family, now that I think of it, were the men: Pop and my dad. Devon asked Pop to tell him stories. He was fascinated with Pop's life as a paper mill worker and a Bayman, and the hard turns it had taken. Pop lost his eldest daughter, my mother's sister, to cancer when she was five years old. It sent him, for a time, careening. It affected my mother in ways I still can't comprehend.

It was only after months of casual drop-ins that I realized Pop was hanging around his house every day in the hope we would come by. He never wanted to miss a chance to spend time with Devon. I started calling him about ten every morning, so he'd know if we were coming by or not.

It was sometime during those months of lunches, when the snow was still two feet deep on the ground, that Dad called me out of the blue. He was breathing heavy. He seemed to be in physical distress.

"We need Devon," he said. "We need him right now."

He and two friends had tracked their yearly moose deep into the woods. It was only after they shot her, though, that they realized how far. They had crossed a small stream, and it was too deep to get the snowmobile across. They had to cut the moose into chunks and carry her, but since two of the three of them were sixty, they knew the pieces would be too heavy. They needed young muscle. Devon had never shot or butchered an animal. I'm pretty sure he'd never seen an animal being butchered. But he pinned their location on GPS and jumped into our car.

My dad has a video from that day. I watch it often. Not because I like seeing grown men reaching into the body cavity of a partially butchered moose, but because I like hearing Devon's voice.

"Oh yes, girl," he says as someone's fists go into the bloody chest cavity. "Get in there." You see him for a second, as the cellphone camera swings up. He makes a face. Tongue out. He shakes his head, like . . . no. Gross. But he's clearly enjoying himself.

The camera pans back down. There is a shocking amount of blood.

"You know what's crazy is, like, you know how in *Star Wars,* the second one, he puts himself in something like this to stay warm, stay alive. The stench! Luke must have been smell blind."

"Oh yeah," someone says. "Oh yeah."

"I think I'm a class-B Bayman now," Devon said with a laugh when he got home. On a normal day, Devon showered twice. He showered for half an hour that night. The stench of dead moose—it's powerful. But that was family: chainsaws, homemade bread, impromptu butcherings. The stench of moose was like a family heirloom, the mark of Murphy. It had only been a few months, and Devon was already one of us.

Why had I ever doubted he would love it here?

Why had I ever doubted anything?

By the first weekend of May, the snow had melted, and the days were bright and clear. People assume the winters are brutal in Newfoundland, but the snow is a warm weighted blanket, and the icicles sparkle on the trees. You snuggle into your blanket, drink hot chocolate, watch the sky drift down. It's lovely. But there's nothing quite like May, when the forests burst with fresh new green, and the rivers flow deep with winter runoff, and you can put away your mittens for only one layer of long sleeves.

We decided to take the dogs for a hike on Marble Mountain. In the winter, Marble was a ski resort. Romy's family had bought the house next to Mom's for its proximity to Marble. Devon's cousin Scott had brought his wife and two young children to ski Marble that winter, and Devon and I visited their rental cabin every night.

"The kids are impossible to get to bed," Scott complained the first night, and Devon said, "Leave it to me."

"Uncle Bebo!" they said when the two of us came up the stairs. "Uncle Bebo!" They were too young to say Uncle Deevs, which is what all the nieces and nephews called him.

Devon jumped right on the bed, while I took a seat in the corner. He teased them for a few minutes, then pushed them into the bathroom to brush their teeth, promising a story when they returned. He did voices as he read from their favorite book. He answered their questions every time they interrupted. In fifteen minutes, they were asleep.

He's gonna be a great dad, I remember thinking.

Now, as we hiked the trails that had only a month before been ski slopes, we talked about baby names. We hiked Marble twice that weekend: on Saturday with my sister, Tamara, and on Sunday with Devon's cousin Brett and his wife, who were living in Corner Brook while she did her medical residency. Brett and Leah were expecting twins, so it's possible we discussed our future children with them on Sunday. But Tamara remembers the conversation, and Brett does, too, so I guess that we talked baby names both days.

Devon liked Frankie, if our first child was a girl. Not short for anything, just Frankie.

For a boy, we were in agreement. We'd name him Oscar. Oscar O'Grady.

On Sunday evening, we celebrated Devon's thirty-second birthday at my mother's house. Devon's actual birthday was the weekend before. We spent that day together, just the two of us. We went for a hike. We took a nap. We showered together, twice. I cooked him his favorite meal, green goddess salad (lol). We went out for ice cream. Devon loved ice cream. We watched a movie, pressed together on the sofa with the dogs. It's so often the little things I smile about, when I smile. Our ordinary moments, our daily lives. A second never seemed wasted when Devon and I were together. I think of Devon every time I think of ice cream.

For his birthday meal at Mom's, Devon requested turkey dinner. Turkey, mashed potatoes, and gravy, a popular weekend meal in Canada, though I hear Americans only eat it at Thanksgiving. Tamara was at the celebration. My mother was there, obviously, working in her kitchen. Pop arrived with a fresh loaf of Devon's favorite bread. He had baked a birthday pie, at Devon's request. Devon insisted pastry was better than cake. We didn't have candles. When I thought about it later, I realized we didn't sing "Happy Birthday," and I hated that. I had one last chance to sing "Happy Birthday" to Devon, and I wasted it. Devon would not have let that happen to anyone else. He was an enthusiastic "Happy Birthday" singer. He had his own rendition, with dramatic flourishes. It was quite good.

At least I got a photograph of Devon with his birthday pie. He was beaming. Pure happiness.

"Sandwiches for days!" he said, laughing as we left with foil-wrapped turkey.

He was in bed with his eye mask, toque, and weighted blanket by eight P.M. "What a great day," he said as he drifted off to sleep. He said that at the end of almost every day.

He was still out on his run when I woke up at six-fifteen the next morning. By the time I showered, got dressed, and came downstairs, he was in the kitchen. He made our morning smoothies: protein powder and fruit for me, gray gunk for himself. I turned down our usual morning shower. I had a couple client meetings, so I'd blown my hair out straight, instead of leaving it curly the way Devon liked it. He tried to kiss me. I turned away. I had my client-meeting lipstick on. These little details, these last mistakes, I hate them. I hate that I cheated Devon of anything.

On the drive to work, Devon was subdued. Not unfriendly, just not his usual exuberant self. He had an important Zoom call in a few hours. It was the last client meeting before his first solo trial, and he was nervous. No, not nervous. Focused. He took time, as always, to laugh and joke with Marsha(mallow), Hilda, April, and the other assistants, then went into his office to prepare. I spent the morning doing paperwork and texting with Reb about meeting up in France during our honeymoon. I told Pop we were too busy, we couldn't come by for lunch. Around ten-thirty, I heard Devon close his door. I could hear him on the Zoom with his clients, but I couldn't hear what he was saying.

It was two minutes before eleven A.M. I remember because that's when my client meeting was scheduled. I was straightening my desk, prepping a few last things, when I heard Devon say, quite clearly, "I'm sorry, I have to pause for a second."

When I stepped out of my office, Devon was stepping into the hall, pulling his office door closed behind him. He leaned against it and looked at me. His eyes were a little wild.

"I can't breathe," he said.

I thought he was having a panic attack. He'd never had one, but . . .

I touched his shoulder. "Let's go into your office."

And then he was on the floor. I don't know how he got there. I didn't see him go down. I just remember Devon sitting with his knees up on the floor of his office, leaning against a filing cabinet.

"Is he okay?" his assistant April asked. "Do you want me to call an ambulance?"

"No, I think he's having a panic attack."

I sat down next to him. I put my arm around him. His head was down. He was inhaling so hard it sounded like moaning. I didn't know it, but his chest cavity was filling up with blood.

"It's okay, Devon," I said. "Relax. You're going to be okay."

He didn't look up. His head was down. His breath was becoming violent, I could see the effort. It sounded almost like snoring.

"I called an ambulance," April said.

I looked at her. Just for a second, I looked at her. Then I looked back at Devon. He had lifted his head. He was looking at me. I saw his face go white. I will never forget it. I see it at night, in the morning, when I beg for him, when I beg for release. I was right there, holding him. I saw his face go white.

He fell. Devon collapsed onto his side. And . . .

I don't know.

I do not know what happened then.

I must have screamed, because suddenly there were people everywhere. There was noise, there was *terror,* but not from Devon. Devon was lying ash-white on his office floor, and I was . . . I don't know what I was doing. I don't know if I was shaking him. If I was grabbing at him. If I was bolt upright with fear. I don't know anything, except that someone pulled me up and pushed me into the conference room. And then my sister, Tamara, was there.

I could hear this . . . rush of sound, like a flock of pigeons bursting into the air. I could hear one of the partners screaming, "Where's the ambulance? Where's the goddamn ambulance!"

I looked at Tamara. I almost asked, but I could see it in her face. I crumpled, right into her arms.

My mother, somehow, she was there. My sister called her. Mom held me close to stop the shaking, but I was screaming, and I couldn't stop. The paramedics, the police, I barely remember them. I think they asked me questions. I remember Devon's best friend, Brett, arriving, because he was screaming, but a hundred miles away. He sounded angry, but looking back, he was probably in shock.

Eventually, when I had shaken myself to bits, and the paramedics were gone, Tamara asked me softly, "Do you want to see him, Laura?"

I nodded, because I couldn't speak.

She led me down the hall to Devon's office. It was littered with needles, bandages, tape, and gloves, the detritus paramedics leave behind. Yellow police tape was across the door. Devon was lying on his back, his arms at his sides, as if asleep without his mask, without his blanket. But he was white. Other people remember him as blue, but I've seen his face a thousand times, it never leaves me for long, and Devon's face was white.

I didn't know it then, but it was the last time I would ever see his face.

My mother pressed her hand against my back. She turned me to go. I was deep inside myself. Unraveling. But it came to me that people were standing silently along both sides of the hall, our coworkers and friends, crying, staring at me in stunned silence as I crawled past them, down the stairs, and out the door.

At home, a delivery box was leaning on the front door. It was a sign I had designed, pink and purple flowers against a white background.

welcome to our wedding

LAURA

and

DEVON

we're so glad you're here

IF WE HAD only had the time. Ten months, perhaps, of knowing it would end so soon . . .

breathe, Laura.

If we had only had ten days . . .

breathe, Laura.

What I wouldn't give for just ten minutes together, ten minutes to hug him tight and tell him everything . . .

A RUPTURED DISSECTING aortic aneurysm. That's what they told me, as if words could explain something so vile. A major blood vessel near Devon's heart tore open and his blood poured out into his chest.

It was sudden. It was vicious. It didn't make sense.

Devon didn't drink. He didn't smoke. He ran every day. He ate carefully. He got exactly eight hours of sleep every night.

He was happy. He was light in his skin. I know he put pressure on himself to be perfect. He wasn't as carefree as people thought. But he was never angry. He was never tightly wound. He was never fretful or red in the face.

He had just turned thirty-two. Thirty-two! He was the healthiest person I knew. His doctor agreed. She told me Devon was her healthiest patient. It made no sense that Devon's body failed him, that it just . . . tore open in one tiny, inch-long space.

What if he had been sick without realizing it, with a bacteria or virus? Could that have played a part? No, they told me. Definitely not.

What about stress? He was stressed about his call. Being a lawyer was stressful for Devon. He never thought he was good at it. Could stress cause a dissecting aortic aneurysm? No.

High blood pressure? Cholesterol? A damaged heart? No, no, and no. Devon's medical tests were perfect.

Then why? We don't know why.

That's what they told me. We don't know. As if that was enough. We know what killed Devon, but we don't know why it happened.

I scoured the internet for medical information. I needed to understand. But what I found seemed iffy, contradictory, scientifically unsound.

I searched out information on what happens when we die. Where do we go? What do we feel? Do we know? Let me break the suspense: You will not find good answers to deep questions online.

I ordered medical textbooks. I read them religiously. I needed to understand how blood vessels worked. Why this tragic breaking occurred. Why it killed him so quickly. I had to know what Devon felt. Was it painful? Was he fully conscious? Did he understand what was happening to him? I had to know if he knew, no matter how much it hurt.

I circled back, again and again, to what I could have done. Chest compression to stop the bleeding? Keep him upright? What if I'd called an ambulance immediately? What if I hadn't tried to calm him, thinking it was a panic attack? Was it a minute before April called the ambulance? Was it five?

Was five minutes the difference between life and death?

It wouldn't have mattered, they told me. If this had happened on an operating table in a hospital, Devon would have died.

I didn't believe them.

My British editor told me her husband had suffered a dissecting aortic aneurysm. She understood, she said, my terror and pain. But her husband lived. A sliding-door moment, she called it. She was being kind, she is very kind, but my chest ripped open, and my mind reeled.

Did Devon's doctors lie to save my feelings? Could Devon have survived, *would he have survived,* if I'd understood better, acted quicker, done everything right?

It was me. That's what I thought on so many of my endless nights, as I lay crying with Devon's face, his ash-white face, inside my head. I was there. I was holding him. He looked at me. His eyes, they *pleaded* with me. They faded. He died.

The question wasn't why. It was how.

How could I have let him go?

Castellina in Chianti

ON THE WEEKEND that should have been our wedding, the two families—mine and Devon's—huddled together at North River. It was a nice idea, the love and comfort of others, but I was resentful, broken. At the barbecue on Saturday, I barely had the strength to stand. But I mentioned to David, Devon's father, that I was thinking of going on our honeymoon alone. I had no intention, in all honesty, of doing it. I couldn't imagine being half so bold. I was only making conversation. But half an hour later, David came up to me, excited and smiling. It was the only time I saw him smile that whole summer.

"I rented you an apartment for a week in Castellina," he said.

Devon and I were not good planners. We had a tendency to wait too long. Living in the moment, I'd like to tell you, but honestly, it was procrastination. England in honor of Sarah, France with Reb, Bath with Romy: Those were on our "yes, we want to" list, though we hadn't booked anything more than a plane ticket to London. But Castellina in Chianti, Italy, was on a different list: the "yes, definitely" list. If we'd been forced to choose one location for the most intimate trip of our lives, it would have been Castellina.

Devon had been to Castellina three times, and he loved it. This wasn't unusual: Devon loved every place he ever went, even the bathroom (according to Bailey). But Castellina was special; he talked about it all the time. The table on the cobblestone street where his family relaxed and people-watched during *la passeggiata,* the traditional evening stroll. The Renaissance palazzo where they rented an apartment. The best burger he'd ever eaten, right at the counter in a butcher's shop. Within weeks of our first kiss, when it was obvious how much we were in love, he said he was going to take me there. He wanted to take our children there. No matter where else we went, Castellina was going to be the heart of our honeymoon.

Sarah had discovered the town when Devon was sixteen. It was the highlight of a family trip to Italy. They went back a few years later, and it was magical again. A few years after that, Devon's parents divorced. I don't know how that played out in the moment, but Sarah and David, who live about a mile apart, have been great friends, to each other and to me, since I've been a part of their lives. They have handled Devon's sudden death together, with kindness and grace. Both still love Castellina, but it's David who has made the town his place.

So it was David and his partner, Jeff, who picked me up at the Florence airport in a Mini Cooper that was, I am shocked to say, even smaller than Lucy's Irish Yaris. I was carsick and claustrophobic by the time we were a few miles out of Florence, but as soon as David turned off the highway, he pulled over, got out, and put the top down. Suddenly, we were in *The Talented Mr. Ripley* (Jude Law version, obviously), whipping along narrow winding roads in our European roadster. In the distance, a line of mountains melted into the sky. Underneath, soft ridges in beige and green. A villa surrounded by Tuscan evergreens, and the straight green lines of hillside vineyards, and the golden glow of wheat. After all the rain in England and Ireland, the sun was shining. The wind was whipping through my hair. I was about to throw up. I don't do well in the back seats of cars. And yet, this was exactly how I dreamed of Italy, the heart-country of romance.

David yelled over the wind, one hand extended to point out Castellina. It was an ancient town, perched so tightly to a high point on the horizon that it seemed as if the hill had spouted spires. In the afternoon sun, the landscape was sfumato, but as we swung closer I saw the terra-cotta roofs, the bright tan walls, an old square tower.

The road does not go into Castellina. It passes by. We parked and walked up an old cobblestone street. David led the way, pointing out a church, a favorite restaurant, the best gelato, another church. The route twisted uphill between elegant stone buildings, between steps and fountains and umbrellaed tables, and I could see it as Devon saw it, the perfect little Italian town, a family place, a happy memory that kept getting better each time he returned. But I was tired from my four weeks on the road, and it was hard to drag my suitcase over the cobblestones. My wrists were deteriorating. My ankles were burning.

Near the top of the hill, we reached the Palazzo Bianciardi. I imagine, at one point, this grand estate was one of the reasons the town was here. At another point, it fell into disrepair. But it had been refurbished and modernized. Half was a hotel; the other half apartments. David rented the same apartment on the fourth floor every summer.

My apartment was in a section owned by David's friend, an older Italian woman. There was no elevator, so I had to carry my suitcase up three flights of stairs. My wrists and ankles were screaming by the time I pushed open the door to my bedroom.

It was so Tuscan, I almost fainted: stone floor, exposed wood ceiling, stone walls, a small window that looked out over vineyards, a distant farmhouse, a patchwork of hills. Like every beautiful thing I saw on my honeymoon alone, it broke my heart.

Oh, Devon, I thought. I wish you were here.

We went to Bar Italia for our afternoon aperitivo. David has a table on a corner, off the square. It's not reserved, but it's his table. He's there every afternoon that he's in town. Devon referred to his father as "the mayor of Castellina," and I saw why. Every few minutes, someone stopped to say hello. David's Italian wasn't great. I'd call it tourist Italian, enough to get by. Jeff, his partner, was a translator. His Italian sounded fluent, although I don't speak a word of Italian, so what do I know? But it was David who did most of the air-kissing and laughing with the locals. This was his special spot on earth. He was so confident and happy here.

I had an Aperol spritz. David and Jeff had beer in tiny glasses. We talked a little, nibbled on salami and cheese. It was the hour of *la passeggiata*. The streets were crowded with walkers. Some were tourists, but there were also young couples in love, parents arm in arm while children scampered around them, older couples stepping carefully in suits and dresses. A group of older women gathered by the entrance to the church. Older men sat fingering Camparis. Devon had described this exact spot to me, this exact moment.

Devon wanted me to see this, I thought. He'd be so happy that I'm here.

IT WAS CLEAR from the first moment Devon and I started spending time together that he adored his sister, Kathleen. She was two years younger, but they seemed like twins. If anything, Devon leaned on Kathleen, not the other way around. Devon was always taking down walls and not knowing how to rebuild them. Kathleen knew how to get things done.

She was an engineer by day, a dancer by night, which sums up her personality. She worked on energy-efficient turbines, I think—who really knows what engineers do?—gave hip-hop dance lessons to children, and danced in a troupe called Mosaic. On one of our first weekends together, Devon took me to one of her performances. I had seen a lot of contemporary dance; it was my brother's major in college. It can be confusing, intentionally so, but Mosaic's art was friendly and inviting. You could feel the kindness. Contemporary dance, I think, is about what it makes you feel.

I was nervous to meet Kathleen. I'm usually nervous with new people, but this was worse than usual, because this was important. When the man you are falling in love with considers someone his platonic other half, it's going to be awkward if she thinks you're lame.

I shouldn't have worried. We hit it off right away. Not because of me, because of her. Kathleen was quieter than Devon, but she shared the qualities that made him special: She was kind. She listened. She was easy to be around.

So I was excited, on the morning after my arrival in Castellina, to ride back to Florence with David and Jeff to pick up Kathleen from the airport. She was exhausted from the overnight flight, but she bounced right out and hugged me.

"I'm so happy to see you, sister," she said.

Kathleen has called me "sister" many times since Devon died. And every time, it sends a frisson down my spine. You're seen, she's telling me. You're valued. Devon chose you. That's forever. You're one of us.

We piled into the Mini Cooper and headed to Siena. We took the back roads. It was raining, so the top was up, and David was whipping around the turns.

"Hey, Dad," Kathleen said. "Can you slow down? Laura isn't feeling well."

I never would have said anything. I'm too polite. So it was nice to have someone notice and speak up for me. That's Kathleen. Just like her brother.

Siena was captivating. It's Tuscany. What do you want me to say?

We were back in Castellina, at David's table, for *la passeggiata*. The conversation started light, but as the rain sprinkled down around us, I noticed the mood becoming tense. Jeff was talking about his former partner, who had died a few years before, when

I realized what was wrong: We had been trying to talk about Devon for the last half hour without talking about Devon at all. Nobody had said his name, but he was there. And once I felt him in our hearts, on our minds but too painful to mention, the pressure began to build: the mathematical moment when the sadness comes crashing over and crushes you, sends you reeling out to sea.

I got up from the table. I know it was rude. I'm sure it was shocking. I didn't even say good-bye or thank you. But I was breaking apart, and I couldn't stay.

I rushed back to my room. I threw myself on the bed.

A minute later, someone knocked on the door. It was Kathleen.

She had been a rock since Devon died. Not just for me, for everyone. Her parents leaned on her. Often, I think, she was the only thing holding them up. The rest of the family leaned on her, to keep them informed, to help them navigate our grief. I leaned on her. I know that. I took advantage of Kathleen's kindness and strength. And she responded, every time. She put my needs first. She was busy: with work, with dance, with friends. Kathleen has many, many friends. But she always had time for a phone call. She always had time to drop by, take me out for a sandwich, tell me what I needed to hear: that Devon's love, his kindness, his influence, would never die.

Frankly, I was worried about her. Kathleen didn't just look exhausted after the flight to Italy; she *always* looked exhausted. She took care of everyone, but she struggled, I think, to take care of herself. And yet, in the four months since Devon died, I had rarely seen her weaken, and I had never seen her break. I remember her looking at me from the doorway, ramrod straight, like always.

And then she crumpled into my arms and fell apart.

We stayed like that for hours. It darkened outside, going from purple to black, as we cried together. It started pouring down rain. We could hear it hitting the overhang. Periodically, the lightning would fork across the window, so sudden and bright it blinded us. And then the boom, shaking the walls.

We talked about Devon. Our connection was so strong, I told her, that I could barely comprehend it. How had we found each other? How had we been so right for each other? How could I go on, knowing I would never have that again?

"I need you to know how much I loved him."

"I know."

"With every part of me, Kathleen. Every part of me, every atom, was in love with him."

"I know."

"You can't be more in love than that. You can't be more in love than what I felt for Devon. I miss him so much. I am so, so sorry I didn't save him."

She hugged me tight. "Sister," she said, "you gave him the happiest years of his life. I never saw him as happy as he was with you."

Life is fucked up, we said. We said it just like that, and then we said it a million different ways, like a curse, like a cry, like a mantra, like a comfort.

Eventually, we fell asleep. Kathleen was staying in the apartment with me, but we had separate beds. That night we slept in the same bed, holding each other, the way my sister, Tamara, had held me for the first week of my widowhood.

It was the best night of my honeymoon.

IT FEELS A little wrong to talk about how close I became with Kathleen. Or maybe not wrong, uncomfortable, because I have a sister, and she's awesome. She's twelve years older than me, and she's a boss, she's tough, she runs massive development projects, she has full-sleeve tattoos, and she's always been there when I need her.

But Tamara and I have drifted apart since Devon's passing, and I know that, just like with Sarah, it's the way our grief collides. Tamara was already going through life-changing trauma in her personal life when Devon died. That's part of it. It's hard for us to find space for each other's pain. But mostly, it's because Tamara was there.

She wasn't there at the moment Devon died. I was there. I was trying to hold him. But Tamara was there a minute later, because she worked two blocks away. She was there when the paramedics arrived. She was there when they said Devon was gone.

It is impossible to explain in words how traumatic those moments were. To see someone you love die suddenly, unexpectedly. To *feel* him slip away. I haven't spoken with my colleagues at Poole Althouse about that morning, and I never will. I haven't spoken to Tamara about it. I know now—I have mostly accepted—that the doctors were telling me the truth, there was nothing I could have done—but the memory of him collapsing still kicks me in the chest so hard that I can't breathe.

It took so many days to write that moment down. I hated doing it. I hated you—just in those moments—because I knew you were probably eager to know what happened to Devon, you were curious for details. It's okay, everyone is. But I didn't want to tell you. I wanted Devon, in those moments, to be mine.

But Tamara was there. She saw it, too.

She texts me all the time. She says, *I miss my sister. Tell me how you're doing.*

I don't write her back enough, and I feel guilty about that. I feel guilty about what I'm doing to everyone all the time. But I know we will get through this. I will get past my pain. Tamara is my sister forever, for always. Tamara, please know, it's only time. It just takes time. I love you still.

THE MORNING AFTER our crying session was bright and clear. Fresh, as the world can only be after a good hard rain. David, Kathleen, and I had breakfast with the elderly owner of the apartment where we were staying. We sat on her deck overlooking the Tuscan hills with strong coffee and Italian pastries that I was tempted by but sadly couldn't eat. A cat lounged languidly in the sunshine in the center of the table. I'm not sure he knew we were there. He certainly didn't care.

The conversation was pleasant but stilted. The woman asked me about myself in rudimentary English, and I tried to answer simply, because of the language barrier. It's very hard, in grief, to answer basic questions without going *there*. My lack of Italian helped; it gave me an excuse to be vague. But after ten or fifteen minutes I began to get the sense the woman didn't know Devon was dead. Finally, David took her aside. It turned out she knew her friend David had lost his son, but she didn't realize I was Devon's fiancée. She thought I was Kathleen's friend.

After breakfast, David drove us to San Gimignano, the City of Towers. Devon was with me every day of my trip. No, every second. In Italy, this absence was heightened, since these were Devon's places, Devon's things. When I passed a SI VENDE sign, "For Sale," I thought of how Devon dreamed of bringing our children here. *Let's buy it,* I could hear him whisper. *Why not?* When I walked down a street, I knew that he had seen it, and I heard him whisper, *Look there, Laura. That artfully rusting water pump. The carvings on the cornice stone. I remember them just like that.* Several times, Kathleen reached out and grabbed my hand at the moment I was missing him most.

But I also felt his presence. Because Devon had been here. Right here. He had sat in this cathedral, he had walked this turning of the road. He had run his hand along the rough stones of this tunnel within the walls. These things were six hundred, eight hundred years old; they had not changed since Devon's visit four years ago.

I started to take a video for TikTok. I started several times. Italy was so picturesque, it felt like a dereliction of my duty not to share it. But I put my phone away. The time I spent with Kathleen and David was so precious, so intimate, I didn't want to share it with the world.

I mean, I'm sharing it now, with you. But sharing here is different. These words are considered and careful, and a book is a reverent space. (I almost said sacred.) TikTok, even at its best, is a frivolous machine.

I put my phone away, took Kathleen's hand, and wandered.

In the afternoon, we stopped at Gelateria Dondoli. Devon always talked about the gelato when he talked about Italy. Now here, in his special place, I ate gelato in his honor every afternoon. I always chose three flavors, so I could try as many as possible, although I suspect Devon would have ordered the same thing every day: affogato, a scoop of vanilla ice cream with coffee poured over it. There were two gelato spots in Castellina, both excellent, but neither compared to Gelateria Dondoli.

A few days later, we drove to Greve. We went to the butcher shop where Devon had told me, many times, about the best burger he had ever eaten, ground fresh and cooked to order, served standing at the counter. As soon as we walked in, I recognized the place. I'd seen a photograph of Devon standing *right there,* with that wall, that sign, that haunch of ham in the background.

They didn't serve the burgers anymore. The butcher shop had gone upscale. Even in an ancient city, things change.

I suppose most visitors remember Italy for its architecture or its museums. I remember those things, too, especially the little window in my bedroom, framing an ever-changing view of Tuscany. But I cherish the memories of the butcher shop and of gelato.

OUR THIRD DAY in Castellina was David's birthday. We went for a stroll and ended up in the city's ancient cemetery. David was almost always upbeat, the mayor of Castellina, the proud tour guide, but I had noticed the moments when he wandered off and, quietly, buried his face in Jeff's shoulder. That morning, he and Jeff stayed in the cemetery, while Kathleen and I headed to the square for gelato. I looked back, and David was shuddering, leaning on Jeff for support.

That evening, David hosted a birthday dinner for twenty friends. He'd planned it after Devon died, probably as a way to ensure he wouldn't be alone. Half the guests had flown in from Canada; the other half were local. The group was too big for the restaurant David wanted, so the owner—a friend—put a long table in the gourmet shop across the street. A private dinner in an old stone room with good friends and fresh pasta and endless wine. What could be more Italian?

I'm not sure David enjoyed it. There was a local boy there, eight years old, and it was his birthday, too. Thank god for that boy, I thought, because he gave David someone to focus on. He forced David to be gregarious, to keep smiling, because he didn't want to spoil the kid's big day, but I could tell a part of him was heavy. I could see the sadness, the hurt down in his bones. He was trying to be the fun-loving, easygoing man he'd been before Devon died, but he wasn't that man anymore.

And I knew him then. I knew David like I knew Sarah, like I knew Kathleen. He wasn't any less devastated than the rest of us. Of course he wasn't, he'd lost his son. He just had a different way of showing it. And my heart broke for him, because I knew his pain.

"I hear you're a lawyer," the woman sitting next to me said.

I looked at her, almost in shock. Her words seemed utterly strange. I mean, I *had been* a lawyer, but I hadn't practiced since

Devon died in my arms. I couldn't, at that moment, imagine going back to my office across the hall from the office where he died. I couldn't conceive of sitting through another divorce negotiation, listening to people who used to love each other argue over scraps.

"Well, then, what do you do?" She kept badgering me with this question. "What are your hobbies? What do you do?"

I understood. It had been four months, she thought I had moved on.

She's rich, I thought. Too rich to understand. Obviously, that's wrong. Rich people suffer as much as poorer people when they lose someone they love. I mean, I went to Europe for six weeks, when many people don't get six days off a year, and I was barely holding on. And I know . . . I know she was just making conversation.

But my god, read the room.

This is a common mistake when dealing with those in grief: putting them on a timeline. Assuming they're healing, because it's been so long, it's *ordinary* to have healed.

Honestly, four months is nothing, especially when a death is unexpected, when it happens in your arms. Nine months, a year, two years: That's nothing to be ashamed of, because there is never anything to be ashamed of. There's no timetable. Not for a tragedy. There's no *right way* to grieve. It's been a year as I write this, and I haven't moved on. I have hobbies now, like pickleball and Pilates. I'm running in the mornings. I'm writing this book. But I mourn Devon every day. I still don't know who I am, or what I want to do, without him.

And that's okay.

Kathleen was also annoyed by the woman's questions. Back in

our room, we started complaining, and after a few minutes, I don't know, I guess we started riffing.

What are your hobbies?

Oh, crying all day.

Staying in bed, curling up in a ball.

Seeing something that reminds me of Devon and totally losing my shit.

Sitting in a coffee shop for two hours, staring at the wall as my coffee goes cold.

Reading the same paragraph of a book ten times without understanding a word.

Not remembering my drive to the dance studio, even though I just parked. Pretty sure I ran two stop signs.

Did I mention the crying?

By then, we were laughing, at each other and the absurdity. I want to thank that woman, sincerely, for giving me a good laugh with my sister. I posted about our "hobbies" later, which shows how much it meant. That post was probably a bad idea. It was messy. But it was human.

And those of us grieving, we're human, after all.

I DIDN'T KNOW what to do as our wedding date approached, and neither did anyone else in Corner Brook. My father had canceled the tent rental. Torn up the menu. Packed up the signs and table decorations. (They are still in his garage.) But June 29 was coming. My family and friends were certain it would sink me.

I don't know whose idea it was, but my father sat on my bed one evening and gently asked if I wanted to go to St. John's to spend the weekend with Devon's family. I did not want to do that. I wanted to do everything else even less. I didn't so much agree as not object.

So on the Friday before the day I was scheduled to marry the man I loved, my family and close friends caravanned seven hours across the island to the southeast corner of Newfoundland. Sarah and Kathleen were staying at Jim and Lucy's cabin. Their neighbors offered my family their house. There were ten of us. I slept in a room with Reb, Janine, and Janine's baby.

Well, *sleep* is not exactly right. Emotionally collapsed.

The next day, Devon's friends and family descended on North River. The house is small, but it has a large deck. The lawn, three times as big as a suburban yard at least, was filled with Devon's family—the people related to him, and the many friends considered as close as family. Kids were running around, chasing dogs. Adults were standing around drinking beer or chasing after their children. The grill was filled with burgers, brauts, and burning vegetables. Music was playing. People were laughing.

I hated it. *Hated it.*

So we're just going to pretend Devon didn't die? We're just going to forget that today is our wedding day? We're just going to have a barbecue, like we did last summer, and the summer before that? We're going to drink and laugh and have a good time? We're going to invite everybody, and we're all going to act like it doesn't matter that Devon isn't here?

I was crushed. Capsized by an iceberg-size wedge of misplaced anger. I felt abandoned, and I felt like Devon had been abandoned. Everyone seemed to be moving on.

Did nobody care about Devon except me?

The next morning, I got up early. Not sunrise early, but early enough. I couldn't sleep. I sloughed into my shorts. I ate a few bites of breakfast with my family. I walked down to the little country road that ran beside North River. The sun was barely up, but there were thirty people standing at the end of Jim and Lucy's driveway.

Over the preceding weeks, there had been a long text discussion (without me) about how to honor Devon. Not a barbecue—that happened spontaneously—but something uniquely Deevs. Someone came up with the idea of a 5K run. Everyone knew Devon loved running.

Sarah drove around the area, using the distance tracker on her GPS to map a route. A friend designed a T-shirt, a line drawing of Devon in his running gear. A few of the shirts read: I LOVE RUNNING, AND I LOVE DEVON (DEVON O'GRADY RUN CLUB EST. 2024).

Most of the shirts, including the one I was wearing, read: I HATE RUNNING, BUT I LOVE DEVON (DEVON O'GRADY RUN CLUB EST. 2024).

Twenty-eight of the thirty people were wearing the special shirts. One of them was Bailey, wearing the I HATE RUNNING version. She asked if she could hold my hand while we ran.

"Of course," I said. "I'd like that."

Bailey's brother, Kai, ran at the front, with Devon's best friend, Brett, who took the lead to make sure everyone went the right way—or because he's ultra competitive. Bailey and I were near the back. At one point, we heard screaming ahead. I looked at Bailey, and she gave me an "I don't know" shrug.

When we rounded the corner, we saw that the road went through an underpass. In the tunnel, where the sound echoed, people were stopping to scream, "I love you, Devon! I miss you, Devon!"

Or in my case, I screamed, "Deeeevoonn!" as long and as loud as I could. Then I looked at Bailey, and we screamed it together as long and as loud as we could: "Deeevvvvvvvoooonnn!"

A few kilometers later, Bailey got tired and she asked me to leave her behind. I went fast the rest of the way. Thanks to running out my fears and frustrations every evening with my father, I was in good shape. Or maybe I had extra energy because I was doing it for Devon.

The course was a little short, Sarah admitted, after we finished. It was only 4.8K. To get to 5K, you had to run up and down the stretch of road outside Jim and Lucy's property. Some people did it.

I didn't bother. Devon would understand, even though he definitely would have run those extra 0.2 kilometers.

ON OUR LAST day in Castellina, Kathleen and I put on our I HATE RUNNING, BUT I LOVE DEVON shirts. I had often worn mine under a jacket or sweater, but Italy was warmer than the British Isles. When I walked around Castellina advertising "I Love Devon," I felt him with me. Laughing. Joking. Pointing out the black metal cock, the symbol of the city, that stood crowing outside the portico of the town wall.

I understood why Devon loved Castellina. I loved modern, boisterous London, but this village was its opposite: old-fashioned, unhurried, peaceful. From every angle there was a gorgeous view: a twisting alley, a glimpse of gardens, an ancient tower. The Palazzo Bianciardi, with its wooden ceilings and table cats, was like stepping into history, or into comforting arms. You know love the moment you experience it. It creeps up on you, and then the power of it knocks you down. I fell in love with Devon as we watched the sunrise at Fort Amherst. I fell in love with Castellina when I felt his spirit here, in the old stone streets, the old stone walls.

The sunset, though, is what you come to a place like Castellina for. And the best place to see the sunset in Castellina, according to Kathleen, was down the one-lane road on the far side of town. That's the joy of traveling with someone familiar with a place: There's always a secret spot. It's always just around a bend.

We lingered a little long with David and Jeff over pasta and Aperol. As we walked toward the square, the sun was already setting. We started to walk fast. Then faster. Soon, we were running in our I HATE RUNNING shirts, out past the last of the buildings, laughing at our foolishness. I was too slow, because my ankles were inflamed and the arthritis had crept into my knees. We weren't going to make it. So as the sun drifted below the Tuscan hills we eased to the shoulder and watched a corner of the sky light up orange beneath a soft ceiling of cloud.

I didn't take a picture. I wanted to preserve the moment in memory, like Fort Amherst. Like Bottle Cove. Like Silent Valley.

I wanted to hold my heart in my hand, with the sunset behind it, and say, Devon, you were right. Time is all we have.

On the walk back to Castellina, I snapped a quick photo. The light was dying; the sky was a streak of orange, pierced by the shadowy Tuscany pines. Back at the town square, Kathleen and I took selfies: laughing, posing. Like sisters. I don't know what we said. It doesn't matter. Everything that needed to be said, we'd told each other already.

I DON'T WANT to leave Castellina without mentioning one other guest at David's birthday party, a friend of his from Toronto. She flew in at the last minute, had to rush from the airport to dinner, but she was there to surprise him when David walked in. She was the only person to bring a present, but it wasn't for David. It was for Kathleen. She sat next to us, at the far end of the table, and gave it to her quietly. I watched as Kathleen fumbled with the paper and the box.

It was a bottle. An empty bottle.

I knew it the second I saw it, because Devon had told me the story. On their second family trip to Castellina, he had wanted to get the woman a gift, so he went into a tourist shop that specialized in limoncello. One brand, out on display on a little table, was shaped like a violin. It wasn't a label. The glass was molded into the instrument. Devon was so proud of buying that bottle of limoncello. He was only fifteen.

This was that bottle, empty now, the liquor long since consumed. I don't know why she had it, but she was gifting back to Kathleen her brother's special gift. David recognized it, too. He held it and simply . . . looked. That is the only time, during my five days in Castellina, that I saw David cry clear, public tears.

Then, as the conversation around the table turned to other things, the woman turned to me. She didn't ask me any questions. She just leaned close and looked me in the eye, like an old friend excited to see me again. She grabbed one of my hands. She said, "Laura"—she didn't ask if I was Laura, she knew—"I have been following you on TikTok. I check your posts every day. I brought you something."

She reached into her bag and pulled out another gift. I looked around, but nobody was watching. I unwrapped it quietly. Inside was a framed piece of paper filled with neat, almost calligraphic writing. It was the lyrics to James Bay's "Hope," the song I had posted about after his concert in London four weeks before. The song had just been released. The lyrics weren't on Spotify or Genius yet. David's friend had listened to it over and over, writing down a few more words each time. Then she had written them out for me, in this gorgeous hand.

I'm not going to say that was the only time I cried clear, public tears. I cried all the time. But never quite like that.

She saw me. Not some version of me built out of her assumptions: the actual me. And she gave, not something she assumed a grieving woman needed, but something with meaning to me.

That's how you treat a person in grief.

That's how I'm trying to treat every person I meet, whether I know them well or not. WWTWFTD. What Would That Woman from Toronto Do?

I DON'T KNOW if that chapter helped you. I don't know if any of this is helping. Traveling. Posting. Writing. What has it done? My grief doesn't feel like something I control. Sometimes it feels like every part of me. Sometimes it feels like an outside force, not part of me at all. So often it feels, even now, that nothing I do matters, the ups and downs are not because I'm *brave,* or *active,* or *speaking my truth,* or *dwelling on it like some mopey girl*. They are merely the twists of a roller coaster I'm forced to ride. And that ride is long and lonely, its track goes on and on, its end—and no, there is no end to grief, I know that now, there's only change—continually out of sight.

But then I look back at my honeymoon alone, and I know that woman's kindness mattered. I know being with David in Italy mattered to us both. Being out of my house, where the air was crushing me. Being in a place Devon loved, with people he loved. It gave me back a piece of him. It gave me back a piece of myself.

And Kathleen. My time in Italy would not have been worth this paper without Kathleen, who can make me laugh, even as she makes me cry. That's sisterhood: when you can laugh and cry with someone at the same time.

In the end, I left Castellina as I arrived: in the back of David's Mini Cooper. The four of us drove to Florence, one last trip. He, Jeff, and Kathleen were flying out in the morning. I was staying in the city for another three days. We spent our last night together at a gorgeous palazzo hotel on the outskirts of town. I woke up early, as the sun was slanting low across the window. Kathleen and I were sharing a room. I know this is going to sound creepy, but I sat and stared at her as she slept.

I thought, What am I going to do without you?

I really didn't know. The anxiety, the sense of doom, was still a part of me.

But a little voice in the back of my head said, *Laura . . . you're going to go on.*

Florence

DAVID GAVE US a quick tour of Florence on the day we drove in. The Duomo. (It's a church.) The Ponte Vecchio. (It's a bridge.) The Palazzo Vecchio. (It's the palace at the end of the bridge.) I saw the statue of David, but not Michelangelo's original, the replica at the Piazzale Michelangelo. This David stands on a high pedestal, looking out over a sweeping view of the city, with its iconic river and big fat church. I've never seen a city, even Bath, that feels more gloriously stuck in time.

After the crew flew back to Canada, I moved into a closet in the center of Florence. City of Sardines, that's Florence. Not because of the fish, because of the confinement. As soon as I stepped out of the door of my hotel, it was wall-to-wall people. The streets are narrow, so as soon as you merge with the traffic, you're swept away. I missed several turns in the crowd, but it didn't matter, I wasn't going anywhere. I was back to my wandering ways.

In Florence, I posted to TikTok, my first posts since the Devon slideshow I pinned to my page in Ireland. The app, which was spamming me constantly with tutorials about getting more people to watch your TikToks, is a hole. Not just a time suck, a great black pit. There's so little time to enjoy it when a video goes viral. There's only pressure to do it again, *right now,* and do it better. If the last video got 4 million views, the next one better get 4.2 million, and if it only gets 3 million, well, that's crushing, that's a disaster, when in reality, it's a blessing. It's an honor to have anyone care about you at all. And yet, TikTok makes it feel like failure.

This time, I just posted a simple video for those who really mattered, my followers, and asked them for tips. I realize, in hindsight, that I posted most when alone. When I was with friends or family, I wanted to spend my time with them, or nap, since spending time with them was emotionally draining. When I was alone, I wanted the companionship, the encouragement, that the better, human parts of social media can provide. There was less response than during my first week in London, the last time I asked for recommendations. Barely posting for four weeks on TikTok is like hibernating for twenty years in the real world. But a few hundred recommendations are plenty.

My three days in Florence were as close as I came to *Eat Pray Love*. It's a different world in "La Bella" ("the Beautiful," the city's actual nickname): art staring at you in every piazza, magnificent buildings with scalloped doorways and iron bolts, curving streets that lead you around the next corner, and the next. Even in September, the city is hot. I put on my sandals. I wore flowing pants like Julia Roberts. I kept my chin up and my eyes on the scrollwork walls, the flowers in the window boxes, the covered passageways that arch across the streets. The Ponte Vecchio, a medieval mall built into a bridge, was here when this city birthed the Renaissance, when Michaelangelo walked these cobblestones—not *some* cobblestones, but these very stones beneath my feet. I saw his David again—you have to see David in Florence, right?—but not at the Galleria dell'Accademia. I didn't go to a single museum on my honeymoon alone. I saw a second copy when I wandered by chance into the piazza where the original had once stood.

I wandered, letting the momentum take me. I drank a lot of wine. Kathleen had tipped me off to the little windows in the wall outside some of the older restaurants. They're closed with a board, so they look like tiny doors, and if you knock, someone will open up and ask you what you want. The wine comes in tiny cups, and once you notice the window, you also notice the small platforms scattered at the edges of the crowd, the kind of tables where you stand and lean. Walk slowly, stop occasionally for a half glass of wine, and you've idled away a pleasant afternoon.

I ate a lot of pizza, and a lot of pasta. Left on my own, I might have been overwhelmed and wandered into a Wingstop. Instead, after a few glasses of wine, I let my GPS lead me into hidden piazzas, where my TikTok followers had recommended a certain restaurant or bar. Italy has a high rate of celiac disease. They have a delicious gluten-free culture. A gluten-free pizza in Canada is almost guaranteed to have a hard or crumbly crust straight off the bottom shelf, but the gluten-free pizzas in Florence were oblong and unround, puffing at the edges, brushed lightly with tomato sauce and splotches of oozing cheese.

I found a little restaurant I loved with pizza, pasta, and arancini, all gluten-free. I sat outside in the shade of ancient buildings, people watching while I ate. I found my way back to that place the next day, and the day after that.

I found a bakery that made an incredible version of that most Italian of treats: gluten-free croissants. I ate mine with a glass of wine.

I sat beside a fountain for hours, sipping wine, although I could never find my way back to it, and I couldn't come close to telling you where it is.

Did I mention that I enjoyed a little wine?

This is not to say I wasn't sad or lonely. There is no victory over grief. Every corner I turned, I saw something to share with Devon. Every evening, sore from arthritis and exhausted from pushing through, I unraveled. I needed to make an appointment for an arthritis infusion as soon as I got home, but our shared insurance was in Devon's name. Every night, I had to explain to a series of people that Devon died, so I couldn't get his approval, but for some reason my appointment was never approved, forcing me to have the same painful, infuriating conversation all over again, and again, and again.

One night I called my dad. I told him I couldn't do it anymore.

"You can do it, Laura," he told me.

I was reading again. I had purchased *Cleopatra and Frankenstein* at Daunt Books, during my first week in London. I tried several times to read it, but my grief wouldn't let me get past the first few pages. It wasn't until Bath with Romy that I managed to get truly started. I was drawn to the book because it was about a young woman who starts over in a new country, but halfway through it turned dark. I've struggled with dark turns since Devon died. I was enjoying a book recently until, three-quarters of the way through, a major character died suddenly of a heart attack. I put it down. I haven't read another page.

But in Florence, in the Old World squalor of my tiny hotel room, I read through pages and pages of a heroine's suicidal ideation, and it was okay. It didn't hurt me.

I wish I'd had a metal bathtub, with a big deep belly. Claw feet.

A rickety tap and peeling paint. The Epsom salts my mother used to ease my arthritis, when I was suffering. A hot towel for my jaw. That would have been the ideal setting for an evening read.

But even without the hot soak, I relaxed. That's what I really did in Florence. For the first time on my honeymoon, I was able to let my anxiety go, to flow like a pair of linen pants, to feel un-overwhelmed by the fact I didn't know where I was going in the next hour, much less with the rest of my life. For the first time on my honeymoon alone, I didn't force myself to get up and experience the world. For the first time since Devon died, the memories of him didn't drown me. Thinking of him gave me, somehow, a place to lean when I was sore. A second soul for my loneliness. I sat on the corner of a busy street with my wine, where no one would notice someone like me, and I watched a couple lean together, whispering against the murmur of the crowd, and I thought, *I wish.*

There is always that *I wish*. It's omnipresent. It's everything.

But in Florence, it was pure. It was a cold sharp cut and not a jagged tear.

Devon, I thought not once but many times, *you would be so proud of me.*

London and Cheltenham

I WENT TO Notting Hill on my first day back in London, a city that started out for me as the loneliest place on earth but had become, over my six weeks of travel, my safe place and home away from home. Justine was supposed to come with me, but she messaged me and canceled. She had found a new place to live, but she was struggling. She was alone with her grief, and that's a hard place to be. She apologized, but she couldn't leave her apartment.

So I walked around Notting Hill alone, looking at the architecture and ducking into the adorable shops. The sun was shining, the crowds were out, and I knew this area. That café. That store. They were TikTok famous. Every influencer who stepped foot in London posted vids from Notting Hill. I wondered if I should be posting as I strolled the street market, where a million TikTokers had gushed over silver trinkets, vintage jackets, a funky lamp. But what of importance could I add?

There was something about Notting Hill that reminded me of home. I felt it, before I realized what it was: the colorful houses. They were charming, worthy of their TikTok fame, but honestly, they weren't as eye-catching as the "Jellybeans" in St. John's. There's a defiant vibrancy in the colorful houses of Newfoundland, a bravado you just don't find in high-end London. When you live on a rainy, fog-covered rock off the coast of nowhere, it makes you strong in a way that living at the center of an empire never can. It makes you appreciate a sharp red, a stinging yellow, a proud blue.

I was meeting one of Devon's ex-girlfriends that night. She had messaged me with a hotel recommendation when I was leaving the Hoxton and was desperate for an affordable room. "You may not know who I am," her message said, "but I was close to Devon a number of years ago."

I knew who she was. Devon had told me about her. She was an artist. A professional photographer. She traveled the world for photo shoots. She took my favorite photo of Kathleen, which is hanging in my house right now. She was one of the relationships Devon's self-doubt had sabotaged.

I was disappointed when her photo shoot ran late and she had to cancel. I wanted to talk about Devon. But she was leaving the next day, probably for some exotic place, which turned out to be true: She was going home to Newfoundland. Maybe next time, we said. Yes, I would love that. But I knew it probably wasn't going to happen. You only get so many chances to cross paths.

Two cancellations, no vids for TikTok, but a positive day. Yes, Devon would have been proud of me.

THE NEXT DAY, at 5:00 P.M., two hours before curtain up, I met an actress and wig designer at the stage door for *Les Mis*. They gave me a backstage tour of the Sondheim Theatre, then we talked in the dressing rooms for a while. They were about my age, very nice, very funny, very interesting. I could have talked with them all night. But eventually I had to take the seat they had arranged for me and watch my new favorite actress walk onstage in my favorite musical. Her wig: spot-on.

The next afternoon, we met at the Picture House after their matinee, since it was around the corner from the Sondheim. The Picture House is a movie theater with restaurants where many West End professionals hang out. The women had memberships to the private club, so I got a backstage pass to that part of their lives, too.

The actress was leaving the production in a couple weeks. She was approaching thirty. She had been in the show three years. It was time, she said, to move on. I could tell it was a hard decision. This was a dream job. But she was excited to see what else was out there for her.

I admitted that, although I was going home to Newfoundland soon, I was thinking of moving to London. I loved the energy, the freedom. I loved the idea of a fresh start. I had friends here now, or at least good acquaintances. The city had taken me in.

They encouraged me to do it. *You're young, Laura. You're smart. Why not?*

I thought: Yeah, Laura, why not? I knew they had reached out to me because of my story, but when we laughed and chatted, when we talked about our lives, it didn't feel like pity. It felt like I had friends in London now.

On my last morning in London, I got up early. I left my hotel and walked down through the sleeping city to the Thames. I intended to watch the sunrise. I wanted to do it for Devon, but I'm not that much of a morning person. By the time I made it to the ramparts along the river, it was close to six A.M. and the sun was above the eastern bank, its light slanting long across the water, the low embunkered buildings, the taller shards that pierced the sky.

It was peaceful. There were only a few people out, strolling or hustling along the waterfront, and the traffic was so intermittent I could hear the river lapping at its walls. The London Eye was motionless; Big Ben in sunlight over my shoulder. I walked along the Embankment. Eventually, I took a seat, waiting, watching, as the city rose around me.

Someone asked me if I thought of Devon. This question misunderstands my grief. I thought of Devon all the time. There were never five minutes in a row on my honeymoon alone when I didn't want to turn to Devon, to speak to Devon, to hold his hand. When I didn't feel his presence at my shoulder, whispering encouragement in my ear. I was aware, at every moment, that he wasn't there.

How to say it? He was a void I filled with memories to keep from falling in. Always, in my mind, in the corner of my heart, there was this empty place, reserved for him.

I missed him all the time. I really, really missed him all the time.

I embraced that sadness. I let it wash over me, there on the bench, in the early morning, alone along the Thames. Sometimes that sadness is a monster wave, pummeling me. Sometimes, a weighted blanket, holding me close. Almost always, it is something in between.

In the ten years my friendship with Romy was conducted online, we mostly messaged about one thing: books. It was a two-person BookTok: a couple friends gushing over their favorite finds, recommending new authors, discussing plot points and characters. I knew Romy better, and loved her more, because of the books she read and loved, even when I disagreed with her opinion, which wasn't often.

Every year, Romy and her mother, the person who taught her to love reading, went to the Cheltenham Literature Festival. I had no idea what this festival was, but I knew it was a highlight of their year. Romy raved about it. She and I loved *Little Fires Everywhere*. We gushed about it for months, in an "oh, yeah, what about this" and "oh my god, remember this" kind of way. Then Romy went to Cheltenham and met the author, Celeste Ng. I was so happy for her. And so jealous. Famous authors never came to Newfoundland. When I decided to honeymoon alone in Europe, Romy insisted I come with her to Cheltenham.

The festival was the first week of October. That was six weeks after my arrival in Europe. My honeymoon was open-ended and only barely planned, but there was no way, I had thought when I arrived at Heathrow anxious and grief-fogged, that I would make it that long. But I made it to France, when I didn't think I'd make it that far, either. And then I made it to Ireland. And Bath. And back to London. By the time I reached Castellina, I could see that Cheltenham was no longer far away. In fact, it was coming up fast. It seemed like the perfect end to my honeymoon alone.

I messaged Romy and told her I would be there.

It will be little surprise to British people, I suspect, that my train ride almost ruined the weekend. The train I was supposed to take to Bath was mysteriously canceled so close to the time of its departure it basically didn't show up. The next train was supposed to have nine cars. It had only five. I had to cram into the luggage cubby, leaning over my bag while that train lurched into *every* stop. It almost felt like they were adding fake stops, just to torture us.

By the time I reached Bath, it was late, and I was tired and sore. But Sam cooked us dinner, and Romy had purchased a kitchen table while I was away in Italy. I'd like to tell you our conversation was high-minded, that we talked about *Cleopatra and Frankenstein* and whatever Romy was reading. Maybe we did. But the thing I remember talking about was *The Secret Lives of Mormon Wives*. I had given it up after a few episodes, because I don't like reality television, but Romy had binged the whole scandalous season.

The next morning, Romy's mother arrived. I hadn't seen her or talked to her since I was a teenager, and you know how some people take you back to a place and time? That was Romy's mom. When I saw her, I felt like I was back in high school.

"Come here. Sit down," she said. "Oh, Laura, tell me about Devon."

Maybe it was because she lost the man she loved unexpectedly. Maybe that's why she understood that this was *exactly* what I wanted to do. Not talk about how I lost Devon. Not how I was feeling. But *about* Devon. The way he looked. The way he talked. The way he laughed. The way he made me feel at Fort Amherst. And Bottle Cove. On our trips to Hawaii and Florida. The way he proposed in *Mississauga*. The silly television shows he liked to watch. The terrible way he cut vegetables, with no two cubes alike. How annoyed he'd get when he lost a game of Qwirkle.

His green peppers. His chickpeas.

His nicknames.

The hikes we took. The house we owned. The work we did. The dogs we loved. The way he went running so early every morning that when I woke up, he was already back and waiting with a cup of coffee and a smoothie just for me.

The way he treated everyone.

The way he made me feel, not just at Fort Amherst or Bottle Cove, but every day. Like he saw me, little old Laura Murphy from Corner Brook, Newfoundland, the most regular woman in the world. The way he loved me like I was special.

The drive was as lovely as the train ride was horrible. The air was crisp. The sun was shining. The trees were flaunting their brilliant gold and orange. (And Romy's mom insisted I take the front seat, so I wasn't carsick.) A few miles from Cheltenham, the traffic began to slow, then finally stopped. We had to park forever away, in a field of infinite cars. Even from there, we could hear the buzz of conversation, the strains of music. We flowed with the crowd of booklovers, their empty bags slung over their shoulders, toward the enormous arch that marked the entrance. The festival was sponsored by *The Times*. Stacks of that morning's newspaper, with a special festival wrap and supplement, sat just inside the arch. I opened a copy—and I was in it.

I had done an interview with *The Times* two weeks before. Romy had been grossed out by many of the articles online, but she almost fell on the floor when she found out I was being interviewed by her favorite newspaper. She and her mother read *The Times* every Sunday morning—not the online edition, the big, fat paper edition. They drank coffee and tea and talked about the articles, sometimes for hours.

I didn't know the piece on me was running until that morning, when Romy noticed it online. I read it on her phone, since I didn't have a subscription. It was a nice article. It included a photo of Devon. I was sad it had to be written; happy with how it turned out. The print version, though, was huge: a two-page spread, with full-color photographs. I stood there at the entrance, with the paper spread wide, and stared. I couldn't believe this was my life.

Eventually, Romy's mother put her arm around me, bringing me back. I folded up my newspaper, stuck it in my bag, and we headed into the festival. The whole town, it seemed, had been turned into a land of books. The shops were decorated. The town hall was an event space for fans. The auditorium was scheduled solid with author panels and readings. Pop-up shops sold bookmarks, reading lights, journals, planners, and other book-anelia. A long hall had been set up on the commons for author events and signings. Hundreds of tables had been set up in the streets, bursting with stacks and stacks of books: children's books, graphic novels, picture books, and every category of adult fiction and nonfiction you could think of. We went into a bookstore—one of the four permanent bookstores in Cheltenham. It had old worn shelves, and wooden ladders you could slide along metal railings, and books piled to the ceiling. And everywhere you went, whether a food truck or a store or an author signing, you heard people in conversation, passionate conversation, about books.

You know how books are an escape from reality? How they transport you to another world? The Cheltenham Literature Festival felt like that. Like another world had been built within our world, an escape for people like me.

Did any of those fellow travelers recognize me from *The Times*? No! Of course not! I was just an ordinary person, talking passionately with my friends. Another booklover smiling, laughing, and enjoying an autumn afternoon.

Nobody special, just someone who was, at least for a moment, perfectly content.

After

FIVE DAYS AFTER Devon died, I hiked up Marble Mountain. This time, instead of walking with the love of my life, I did it with close family and friends. The day was clear but cloudy, unlike our last sunny weekend together, when Devon and I discussed our future children's names. The mood was somber. Even the dogs were subdued. Maybe I talked on the way up, I don't remember. The hike was more than an hour; I suppose we must have said something. Near the top, I took the backpack that everyone else had been taking turns carrying. The backpack that held Devon's ashes. I put it on. It was my first, and maybe only, conscious act. I started jogging and then, before I realized what I was doing, I was running as hard as I could. I looked over, and my father was running beside me.

At the top, he gave me a hug. I'm not sure I felt it. I'm not sure it wasn't the only thing holding me up. Someone opened two bottles of champagne. I think it was David, Devon's father. The hike was his idea. We each took a glass. We toasted Devon: my mother and father, his mother and father, my sister, his sister, my brother, our friends Leah and Brett. Pop was in his eighties. We didn't think he'd make it, but he was there. Pop drank a toast to Devon, his first drink of alcohol since his first grandchild was born.

So beautiful in the telling.

So painful in my heart.

By the time I got home from my honeymoon five months later, my parents had sold the house where Devon and I had planned to build our lives. I asked them to do it. I knew I needed to move, but it was too hard for me to sell our dream, to deal with the cleaning and showing, the negotiating, the demands. My bed—our bed—was in the spare bedroom at my father's house. Beside it was the backpack I had carried to the top of Marble Mountain. Devon's ashes were still inside.

It was devastating. Absolutely devastating. I hugged the backpack to my chest and curled up on the bed. I had slept that way, wrapped around Devon's ashes, in the weeks after his death. I felt the same crushing emptiness now, like a heavy stone on my chest. Like the sharp pain in my abdomen that made me hope, in the days after Devon died, that I was going to join him.

I was miserable in my first weeks back from Europe. I cannot lie to you about that. The pain I'd been holding at bay while overseas came crashing down on me, and I struggled with the darkness. It didn't help that it was the shoulder season in Newfoundland, a six-week period of short days and cold driving rains before the gorgeous snows of winter.

Pop came by. He sat on the edge of my bed. He told me he never sat in the chair Devon sat in when he came to visit him. He often rested his hand on the top of that chair, he said, and thought of Devon, but he couldn't bring himself to pull it out from the table. I knew that feeling. Pop didn't want to sully a memory. He didn't want to obscure the things Devon had done. Who he was. What he meant.

I knew I had to get out of Corner Brook, this time for good. I looked into moving to London, but in the end it was too far, and too complicated with the dogs. I took a trip to Toronto with my sister, Tamara, to see Taylor Swift. (Tamara repped the *Reputation* era. I dressed for *The Tortured Poets Department*. The album came out a few weeks before Devon died.) I spent Christmas with my family. Then I moved to St. John's.

It hasn't been entirely smooth. The first anniversary of Devon's birthday, then his death date, then our wedding date, knocked me flat. The one-year mark is hard. Everyone told me that, and it's true. The loss seems far enough away in time that it doesn't make sense for it to feel so close and sharp. My resolve collapsed. I crawled back to my father for a week.

That is the reality of grief. There is no end. There is no *healed*. Not as one clear moment in time. Not because you *want to*. Learning to live with joy again is a process, a journey of stops and starts, at best a torn and jagged line.

But step by step, I am embracing my life as it is now. I posted on TikTok a few times after I returned, but it didn't feel authentic to my emotional state. Instead, I poured my soul into this book, which is its own emotional journey. It's a lonely task, but I haven't been alone. I have Leni and Chewy, my beloved bernedoodles. When I hug Chewy deeply, I smell Devon in his fur. I remember him sliding up Devon's chest, rolling his eyes, and stretching his tongue to lick at his nose. It's the little things. It's the big things. Even now, it's everything.

I have my friends from London, and many of the grieving women who contacted me online. We live in a connected world, and connection matters, even if it's only once or twice a month. I text regularly with Justine, who has moved to a new country for a fresh start. She is better. Not there yet, but better.

I have Romy and Reb, who may not live near me, but because of their part in my journey they are closer to my heart than they had been before.

I have Kathleen, who lives a few blocks away, and whose presence brings me comfort every time I see her.

I have a great group of friends here in St. John's. They invite me to dinner. We play pickleball. We hike. Every sixth day of the month—the date Devon died—we gather for a run. I didn't run in Europe, and I've failed to run as much as I intended in St. John's, but I don't miss the sixth. Sarah and Kathleen are always there. Bailey and her brother, Kai, have come. There are usually ten to fifteen of us, in our I HATE RUNNING, BUT I LOVE DEVON shirts, and we run together. We run for one another. We run for Devon.

The tension I felt around Sarah—my fear of a hurt too big to handle—was lingering when I moved to St. John's, but it has eased. Part of that was time. A big part was this book. I talked to Sarah about everything I was writing, about my fear of hurting her and Devon. I confessed that I was including the hard parts. Honesty was necessary, but it also felt like a betrayal. It wasn't what I wanted the world to know.

"Don't worry, Laura," Sarah said. "There's nothing to be afraid of. I am proud of the way you and Devon handled that situation. Laura, I hope you know, I am so proud of you."

And just like that, there was another letting go. Another loosening of the ropes that bound my heart. I put them there. I bound myself. She cut me free. And now Sarah and I are closer than ever.

It's my female friendships, I realize now, that have brought me back to life. It is my female friends, not mountains in Ireland or wine in Florence, that bring me peace and joy, not only now but in the years to come.

Kelsey Mulcahy posted something on her TikTok account that has stuck with me through this journey, something her doctor told her early in her grief: "Not many people get to experience the privilege of a loss this great, and one day you will understand what I mean."

I didn't like that at first, and I'm still not sure I agree. This loss is not a privilege. But I understand what she meant. Losing Devon stripped me down to nothing. It made me examine everything. I had to rebuild my life, maybe not from scratch, but from what felt like ruin.

And I like the Laura Murphy I have become. She's stronger. She's more open with her feelings and willing to say what she thinks. She doesn't worry as much about other people's opinions, which is why she was able to post those vulnerable TikToks and write this book. I didn't become that Laura Murphy by chance. I grew into her because I went, because I *acted*. I was afraid. This has nothing to do with not being afraid. I failed and flubbed so many days away. But I learned to be my best, to believe in myself, on my honeymoon alone.

I used to think I wanted a perfect life. Dream job as a lawyer. Picture-perfect house. Handsome husband. Happy family. I worked so hard, and I worried so much. But now I know there is no perfect life. The most perfect thing I ever had was the thing I worked for the least. With Devon, all I had to do was be myself.

And now I can see the truth: That's all I ever needed to be.

Pop told me, a few days ago, that he had begun to sit again in

Devon's chair. I suppose I'm meant to find some symbolism in that, to say we all move on, time heals. But I don't feel that way. I don't want to ever sit in Devon's chair.

I keep his ashes near my bed. I wear his Muhammad Ali sweatshirt, and I hug myself, almost as if I am hugging him, and cry. I hung his first gift in my bedroom, the photograph that reads, "i love you still." I look at it every night. The word *still*. The way it's at the end, not in the middle. Not an angry *still,* not a *despite it all,* but a longing for what is gone.

When I see that *still* I feel Devon's arms around me. I feel him whisper, "I'm here. I see you. What you're doing is beautiful, honeybee. I always knew you could."

I know I feel his love, even now, because Devon taught me how to love myself.

And I understand, as I never did before, that the goal of this journey is not the end of pain. I will always hurt for Devon. I *want* to always hurt for Devon. But I am able to wrap myself in his memory and find comfort in it. I find strength in knowing that I opened my heart, and I let the hurt become a part of me. I can't hold on to the joy of loving Devon without the pain of losing him, because they are intertwined, so I embrace them both.

I embrace, with both arms, this life I'm living now.

It's funny, but now that I'm at the end of this conversation, I find myself thinking of a tiny oddness that gnawed at me when Devon and I lived in St. John's. One tiny . . . imbalance, I guess you'd say. I noticed that his brother-cousins often asked Devon for help, and he dropped everything to help them, no matter what we were doing. Even if it was the middle of the night, even if we were having a romantic night in, Devon would rush to help his brothers, gladly, devotedly. But Devon never asked for their help in return.

I got an explanation, inadvertently, when I sat down to talk with his cousin Brett for this book. Brett had been through everything with Devon. He was one of the childhood friends who hurt him when he turned away. And yet, he was closer to Devon in his last year of life than anyone, except for me. He lived a few blocks from us in Corner Brook; he was there the morning Devon died. His wife, Leah, was pregnant with twins at the time. They named one of their sons Beau Devon. They were afraid, for a few months, that Beau Devon wouldn't make it. He was premature and underweight. But Devon's name lives on in that adorable little boy.

"Devo had a lot of girlfriends," Brett told me. That's what the brothers called him, Devo. "Even as a little kid, Devo was a romantic."

At seven, all Devon wanted was a girlfriend. Also, to play basketball. But mostly, a girlfriend. He talked about his first crush incessantly. When her family moved away, he was destroyed. He was sure he'd missed his chance at love. He was in the third grade.

The next year, he developed an even bigger crush—on his teacher. His family still laughs about that. Devon laughed about it, too. He wasn't ashamed. He kinda loved how foolish he'd been.

"I knew it was different with you," Brett told me, "because he didn't talk about it."

With his other girlfriends, Devon was constantly texting his brothers, wanting to get together, asking them questions. He would come by their houses late at night and pick them up. They'd park somewhere and talk. He'd ask them what was wrong with him. Why couldn't he do things right? Why couldn't he figure out the secret? Why didn't he feel the way he was supposed to feel?

"With you," Brett said, "Devo went silent. He disappeared. That's how I knew it was real. Laura, you were what Devon had always wanted."

It matters to me to know that what I shared with Devon was special to him. That he was at peace with me, as he had never been before. That I gave him as much as he gave me, even though he gave me everything. It's a gift that I will cherish always. It's the kernel of peace from which my vibrant future life grows.

I'll say it again, as I said at the beginning: I hope you find someone to love you the way Devon loved me. I hope you get the chance to love someone as deeply as I love Devon.

I hope, I pray, you live a long and happy life, as Devon would have wanted for you, and that it's full of sunrises and ice cream.

My sweet Dev,

i love you still.

Oh, what a valiant roar . . .
Our field of dreams engulfed in fire . . .
And I'll still see it, until I die
You're the loss of my life.

—Taylor Swift, "loml" (Love of My Life)

Acknowledgments

Thank you to my editor, Maya Ziv, and the team at Dutton: Justina Vasquez, John Parsley, Stephanie Cooper, Isabel DaSilva, Amanda Walker, Jamie Knapp, Melissa Solis, Alice Dalrymple, Nancy Resnick, and Clare Shearer. You were incredibly understanding and kind.

To Bret and my agent, Daniel Greenberg, for believing in me.

To my dad, who supports me every day.

To Kathleen, Sarah, and David, who gave me comfort and strength (literal and metaphorical) through the hard winter when I was writing this book, and for raising my favorite person in the world.

To Reb, who encouraged me to get on that plane and post a TikTok, and for always being my safe place to land.

To everyone who talked with me about Devon for this book. You told me so much I didn't know.

Thank you to everyone in my life for bearing with me, which I know was not always easy, and for bravely trying to understand what I was experiencing. Shout-out to my friends for remaining my friends when I ghosted you for weeks at a time while writing this book.

Thank you to my entire family, Devon's and my own, for always loving me and trusting me with memories most precious.

And most of all, I want to thank you, Devon, for giving me enough love in three years to last a lifetime.

About the Authors

Laura Murphy intended to chronicle her solo honeymoon on TikTok for family and friends, but instead, millions cheered for her as she explored if "life was still worth living" after devastating loss. A lifelong booklover, she spent the next year focused on healing and writing, before resuming her career as a lawyer. Murphy lives in St. John's, Newfoundland, with her two dogs (yes, you can ask her for pictures).

Bret Witter has cowritten nine *New York Times* bestsellers, including two number-one bestsellers. He lives in Philadelphia.